Gates of Prayer
שערי תפלה לנוער
for Young People

Services for Shabbat and Weekdays

Created by
Rabbi Roy A. Walter
Rabbi Kenneth D. Roseman

Illustrated by
Brad Gaber

Edited by
Rabbi Elyse Frishman

CENTRAL CONFERENCE OF AMERICAN RABBIS
5757 NEW YORK 1997

The publication of this prayer book is made possible by the generosity of the Westchester Reform Temple in honor of their beloved rabbi

Jack Stern

Library of Congress Cataloging-in-Publication Data

Walter, Roy

Gates of prayer for young people / written by Roy Walter ... [et al.] ; illustrated by Brad Gaber.

p. cm.

Adaptation of the prayer book published by the Central Conference of American Rabbis.

ISBN 0-88123-045-6

1. Reform Judaism–Prayer books and devotions–Juvenile literature. [1. Reform Judaism–Prayer books and devotions. 2. Judaism–Prayer books and devotions. 3. Prayer books and devotions.] I. Gaber, Brad, ill. II. Siddur (Reform, Central Conference of American Rabbis) III. Title.

BM674.36.W35 1994

296.4–dc20 94-5003

CIP

AC

 Composed at Nostradamus Advertising by Warren Wolfsohn and Wendy Wolf, with help from Dr. Yehiel Hayon and Amy Helfman.

01 2000 1999 98 97 10 9 8 7 6 5 4 3 2 1

DESIGNED BY *Barry Nostradamus Sher*

Contents

Preface ix
A Note to Parents xiii

For Younger Children

Candle Blessing 3

Evening Service I: ***For Shabbat or Weekdays***

Opening Blessings 5
Sh'ma and Its Blessings 6
T'filah 17

Evening Service II: ***For Shabbat or Weekdays***

Opening Blessings 27
Sh'ma and Its Blessings 28
T'filah 38

Morning Service I: ***For Shabbat or Weekdays***

Opening Blessings 49
Sh'ma and Its Blessings 51
T'filah 58

Morning Service II: ***For Shabbat or Weekdays***

Opening Blessings 67
Sh'ma and Its Blessings 68
T'filah 76

Seder K'ri-at Ha-Torah 89

Closing Prayers 99

Kiddush 105

For Older Children

"Words of Our Mouths, Thoughts of Our Hearts"
A Service for Shabbat and Weekdays

Opening 111
Candle Blessing 112
Sh'ma and Its Blessings 113
T'filah 122
Seder K'ri-at Ha-Torah 134
Closing Prayers 141

Songs 147

For Younger Children

Candle Blessing for Shabbat

Evening Service I
For Shabbat or Weekdays

Evening Service II
For Shabbat or Weekdays

Morning Service I
For Shabbat or Weekdays

Morning Service II
For Shabbat or Weekdays

For Older Children

"Words of Our Mouths, Thoughts of Our Hearts"
A Service for Shabbat and Weekdays

For Everyone

Songs

ix PREFACE	xiii A NOTE TO PARENTS				
3 CANDLE BLESSING					
5 OPENING BLESSINGS	6 SH'MA AND ITS BLESSINGS	17 T'FILAH	89 SEDER K'RI-AT HA-TORAH	99 CLOSING PRAYERS	105 KIDDUSH
27 OPENING BLESSINGS	28 SH'MA AND ITS BLESSINGS	38 T'FILAH	89 SEDER K'RI-AT HA-TORAH	99 CLOSING PRAYERS	105 KIDDUSH
49 OPENING BLESSINGS	51 SH'MA AND ITS BLESSINGS	58 T'FILAH	89 SEDER K'RI-AT HA-TORAH	99 CLOSING PRAYERS	105 KIDDUSH
67 OPENING BLESSINGS	68 SH'MA AND ITS BLESSINGS	76 T'FILAH	89 SEDER K'RI-AT HA-TORAH	99 CLOSING PRAYERS	105 KIDDUSH
111 OPENING	113 SH'MA AND ITS BLESSINGS	122 T'FILAH	134 SEDER K'RI-AT HA-TORAH	141 CLOSING PRAYERS	105 KIDDUSH
147 SONGS					

Illustrations

Cover
At the bottom of the page, *Siddur* is spelled in Hebrew with flowers. The text of the traditional *Siddur*, or prayerbook, follows the pattern of creation, revelation, and redemption. The sky, land, and trees represent creation. The Mountain (Sinai) represents revelation and the roads leading from it represent redemption. There are also eighteen children in the painting: eighteen in Hebrew is *chai*, which also means life.

For Younger Children—Part Title 1

Shabbat Candle Blessing 3
Three stars at the top of the page show the beginning of Shabbat. The candles separate the Shabbat from the rest of the week.

Evening Service 5

Bar'chu 6
The pink triangle of the Magein David represents people reaching up to God. The yellow triangle represents God reaching down to us. The silver trumpets were used in the ancient temple to call the people to worship. Although blown by the Levites (pink), the sound becomes holy (yellow) when we praise God.

V'ahavta 10
The Hebrew letters of the V'ahavta wrap around the left hand like T'filin, "Bind them as a sign upon your hand."

God's Protection 15
The right hand of God will protect us, even in sleep.

Asking 22
The rainbow of God's love emanates from the Torah as the waters of God's bounty flow off of the page and into the world.

Evening Service 27

Bar'chu 28

Redemption 34
The Magein David of freedom, made from an Egyptian pyramid, (symbolizing slavery), and wheat, (symbolizing matzo, the bread of redemption).

Avot 39
The shield of Abraham, "God, You are our protector," with the rainbow of the covenant above.

Silent Prayer 46
The Eternal is my rock and my redeemer.

Morning Service 49

Bar'chu 51

Sh'ma / V'ahvta 54
A father and daughter studying this prayer book. "Teach them faithfully (these words) to your children."

K'dusha 60
The sun symbolizes the light of God, who is hidden. The rays of the sun touch the earth and make it holy, "KADOSH."

Peace 64
The light of God shines on the dove and casts a shadow of peace across the world.

Morning Service 67

Creation 69
God created the world, even the tiny ant in the foreground.

Redemption 74
The world, centered on Israel, held prisoner behind the bars of a jail cell, waits for redemption.

Asking 83
Eighteen children and eighteen adults (a double "chai") holding hands around the world with a ray of sunshine touching Israel.

Torah Service 89

Torah Blessings 92–93
A rabbi reading Torah, as the first words from each of the five books flow out into the congregation and into the world.

Returning the Torah 97
The Torah as "the tree of life" turned upside down with its roots in heaven, (based on a midrash), and attributes of God flowing through to us. There are thirteen values shown, as Maimonides described thirteen attributes of God.

Kiddush 105
The blessing over wine separates the Shabbat from the rest of the week, as the dark Magein David is separate from the white page. This is also a symbol of God separating the light from the darkness, just before the first Shabbat.

For Older Children—Part Title 109

Words of Our Mouths, Thoughts of Our Hearts 111
Like a whisper of wings.

Creation 116
Paraphrased from the Midrash, "The Torah is the blueprint for the world." Also depicted are the sun, the moon and stars; lilies, oaks and trout; tiger and bear; sparrows, hawk and ape.

Avot 122
Abraham & Sarah; Isaac & Rebekah; Jacob, Leah & Rachel, (who began the covenant with God), shown in the foreground. The twelve tribes of Israel (sons of Jacob), represented by Jews in the middle ages, (who continued the covenant); and all of present day Jews, (without whom there would be no covenant), forming the word "AVOT," (generations).

Jerusalem 129
The Jerusalem above (spiritual world), and the Jerusalem below (real world), represented by the 3000 year old city of Kings David and Solomon, and the current city of today.

Torah 135
Hagbaha—a Rabbi holding the open Torah scroll and showing it to the congregation as it is about to be returned to the Ark.

Closing Prayers 142
Children join hands as God's World hovers just on the border.

Songs 145
This illustration shows traditional instruments used to accompany songs: harp, flute and tambourine; plus a shofar, to heed.

End Papers ....Inside cover
In general, this illustration is a compilation of the images used throughout this book. The most noticeable exception is the stained glass window on the left-hand side of the spread. The large white circles are taken directly from windows in the Prague Synagogue and symbolize Abraham and Sarah, Isaac and Rebekah, Jacob, Leah and Rachel. Within the circles, the spouses are spiralled in a loving embrace. The twelve small white circles represent the tribes of Israel (sons of Jacob). The rainbow above is God's protecting shield, the covenant with Abraham through all generations.

Preface

Just as a locked gate cannot be entered without a key, so the world of prayer requires an opening tool if children are to make their way into it effectively. Young people cannot be expected to apprehend the full depth of religious experience or to realize the spiritual fullness of worship without the thoughtful and intentional assistance of adults.

Some years ago, the Central Conference of American Rabbis inaugurated a project to help our children and their elders discover such a key. Our goal was to combine contemporary child development theory, educational insights and language-acquisition practice with a sensitive and literate rendition of liberal Jewish worship that would open the gates of prayer for our young people.

Early in this process, we concluded that one service or even one volume of services would not suffice; our children span too wide a chronological spectrum for a single choice of language or ideas to be equally meaningful to all of them. We determined to create an age-graded series of liturgical materials which could be used in synagogues, schools and homes to help our children grow in religious sensibility and, eventually, by the age of Bar or Bat Mitzvah, begin using our adult liturgies with an understanding, comfort and appreciation that had hitherto been unavailable.

The first two volumes of this series, *Gates of Wonder* and *Gates of Awe,* by Rabbi Howard Bogot, Rabbi Robert Orkand and Joyce Orkand, speak to the needs of our youngest children, those who cannot yet read. Beautiful and inspiring art was created by Neil Waldman. These "prayer-readiness" books can be read to young children by adults; the ideas and values contained in them constitute marvelous openings for discussion in class, at the dining room table or at bedtime.

This present volume is the second key to the gates of meaningful religious worship. Rabbi Roy Walter has created a series of Shabbat and weekday services for children in the lower primary grades (grades 1–3, approximately), while this writer has provided a more traditional, combination Shabbat and weekday service for those in upper grades (grades 4–6, approximately). Using more complex syntax, richer language, more advanced intellectual content and the wonderful artistic renditions by Brad Gaber, these services lead in a variety of ways to the use of the adult siddur of Reform Judaism, *Gates of Prayer,* or its gender-sensitive companion, *Gates of Prayer for Shabbat and Weekdays.* We anticipate publishing a companion machzor for the High Holy Days for children of these ages in the near future.

I wish to extend my gratitude to the following:

Dr. David Elkind, Tufts University, who provided deep insight into the religious aspects of child development.

Rabbi Elisabeth Stern, Jean Kaplan, Carole Robbertson and Tana Tenenholtz of Temple Shalom whose counsel and additional work refined the service.

The children and parents of Temple Shalom who allowed themselves to be the subjects upon whom these words were repeatedly tried out and whose responses were invaluable.

Helen Roseman of blessed memory, reading and language teacher, who constantly supported this work and offered many creative and valuable suggestions.

We dedicate this volume to our children, with the prayer that, given the key to the gates, they will more easily enter the world of religious experience and thereby enrich and sanctify their lives.

Kenneth D. Roseman
Chair, Committee on Children's Liturgy

The Early Primary Services were developed over a period of several years, with the help and support of a great many people whose contributions I would like to acknowledge:

Rimma Tulchinski, who served as my secretary during the time these services were being written and who diligently kept track of draft after draft and faithfully preserved all comments and changes, and Brenda Nasser, my current secretary, who has done the same with the last drafts.

Dr. Jerome Berryman, Canon Educator of Christ Church Cathedral in Houston, who has wide experience in children's liturgy, read the manuscript and made many suggestions regarding language and imagery that have been incorporated into the manuscript.

Phil and Ilene Garoon, special, dear friends, who generously provided me with a haven to isolate myself from the demands of my everyday Rabbinate and create the focus necessary for creative thinking.

And, finally, the children and adults of Congregation Emanu El who have appreciated and encouraged the creation of special children's liturgy and inspired me to continue trying to stir the hearts of young people to worship.

To all of these wonderful people, I offer my thanks for their contribution to the creation of these worship services.

Roy Walter
Rabbi, Congregation Emanu El
Houston, Texas

The CCAR Press extends its gratitude to Rabbi Elyse Frishman, who edited this volume with a profound sensitivity to the nuances of language. Her patience and devotion have improved this prayerbook in innumerable ways. Sarah Morgan and Judith Redlener, Managing Editors for the CCAR Press, managed the project's myriad of details with consummate skill. Our thanks, too, to Rabbi Elliot L. Stevens for his unfailing support through the years, as the scope of the CCAR's children's liturgy project changed and expanded. Rabbis H. Leonard Poller, Peter Knobel, Stephen Pearce and Robert Levine, as chairs of the CCAR's Liturgy or Publications Committees, have all helped with editorial development, as have Rabbis Howard Bogot, Adam Fisher and Daniel Freelander, and Cantor Jeffrey Klepper. Numerous educators and specialists in music, language, and child development have our gratitude for their contributions of time and expertise along the way. We also thank Barry Nostradamus Sher, whose innovative design bridges the gap between liturgy and pedagogy.

A Note to Parents

The services in this prayerbook have been prepared especially for your children. They are age-appropriate, some for younger children, some for slightly older young people. It is likely that you will be sharing these services with your children, and we want to help you make these religious moments very special for your family.

When you and your children talk about going to services and joining in prayer together, we hope you will help them to recognize and enhance the attitudes and values that are reflected in the services of this Siddur (and in all Jewish prayer), even after you leave the sanctuary and close this book. We hope the gates will remain open.

You can help your children understand that prayer is not a foreign language, but a form of conversation with God, with ourselves, and with those around us. In the Kaddish, for example, we let God and those around us know that we are mourners. This form of conversation is a very special, remarkable and holy way of thinking and communicating with ourselves and with God.

Children also need to know that prayer is a way of connecting—with God, with the Jewish people both past and present, with Jewish history, and with nature. By helping your child make these connections, you will help engender a sense of awe, holiness, humility, purpose, and destiny, all integral parts of Jewish worship, faith and life.

The idea of k'lal Yisrael, being connected to and involved with the people and the land of Israel, will also give your children a sense of the history and the tradition to which they belong.

Thankfulness is another essential ingredient in Jewish piety. Try to help your children focus on and recognize the things in their lives for which they should be grateful (our families, nature, etc.) and why they should be grateful for them.

Torah is another important element of Jewish worship. You may want to explain that acquiring knowledge, treasuring the life of the mind, and respecting the gift of intelligence that God has bestowed upon us are Jewish religious values. Jews express these values through reading the Torah, and through the eternal quest for wisdom. The stories of the Torah which we read or which the rabbi preaches can help us in our pursuit of wisdom.

The ideas of Jewish ethics and morality also lend themselves to an ongoing dialogue between you and your children. You can find values and ethics expressed on almost every page of this Siddur. You may want to discuss with them why Jews have been at the forefront of freedom movements, and what the Exodus and our people's search for freedom mean. You may want to explain that, as Jews, we know what it is to be poor and oppressed and disadvantaged, so we have participated in virtually every effort to create a more humane society, and we have always sought the highest standards of personal and public morality.

Children will have many, many questions about God, and you may not be able to answer all of them. No one can. Share your thoughts, and even your own questions about God with your children. Explore God together rather than trying to offer a once-for-all-time answer. We hope this book will open the door to such a dialogue.

A prayerbook, this prayerbook, is a start. It offers you a wonderful opportunity to engage your children in conversation, to help them grow as people and as Jews. Most of all, it is a symbol of Jewish hope—the hope that we can remake our world into the world that God and we would like to create. We hope you will help your children become partners with God in fashioning a better world.

For Younger Children

Candle Blessing for Shabbat

3
CANDLE BLESSING

God began the world by saying,
"Let there be light."

We begin Shabbat with candlelight,
saying: "Baruch ata, Adonai."

God finished creating the world
by making Shabbat a holy day.

We make Shabbat
a holy day for ourselves.

May the warm glow of these candles
remind us of God's light.

And may this Shabbat be
a special, holy time for us.

Baruch ata,	בָּרוּךְ אַתָּה,
Adonai Eloheinu,	יי אֱלֹהֵינוּ,
melech ha-olam,	מֶלֶךְ הָעוֹלָם,
asher kid'shanu	אֲשֶׁר קִדְּשָׁנוּ
b'mitzvotav	בְּמִצְוֹתָיו
v'tzivanu l'hadlik	וְצִוָּנוּ לְהַדְלִיק
neir shel Shabbat.	נֵר שֶׁל שַׁבָּת.

We praise You, God,
for the mitzvah to
light Shabbat candles.

For Shabbat or Weekdays

Evening Service I

O God, help us do what is important:

To love our parents
and our family,

To share what we have
with others,

To be kind to people
who need help,

To be honest and fair,

To learn more about You,
and what You want us to do.

Sh'ma and Its Blessings
שְׁמַע וּבִרְכוֹתֶיהָ

PLEASE RISE

Bar'chu et Adonai ham'vorach.	בָּרְכוּ אֶת־יי הַמְבֹרָךְ!
Baruch Adonai *ham'vorach* *l'olam va-ed.*	בָּרוּךְ יי הַמְבֹרָךְ לְעוֹלָם וָעֶד!

Baruch ata,	בָּרוּךְ אַתָּה,
Adonai Eloheinu,	יי אֱלֹהֵינוּ,
melech ha-olam,	מֶלֶךְ הָעוֹלָם,
asher bid'varo	אֲשֶׁר בִּדְבָרוֹ
ma-ariv aravim.	מַעֲרִיב עֲרָבִים.

Your world is like a puzzle, God,
and all the pieces fit together.

The sun lights up the earth by day.

Moon and stars glow at night.

Icy winds make us shiver in winter.

Gentle winds cool us in summer.

Red and brown leaves
crunch beneath us in fall.

Flowers smell sweet in the spring.

Awake is a time to play and learn and love.

Asleep is a chance to rest and grow.

Your world is like a puzzle, God,
and all the pieces fit together.

Baruch ata, Adonai,	בָּרוּךְ אַתָּה, יי,
hama-ariv aravim.	הַמַּעֲרִיב עֲרָבִים.

We praise You, Eternal God.

You created the world
and all its wonderful pieces.

Ahavat olam	אַהֲבַת עוֹלָם
Beit Yisra-eil	בֵּית יִשְׂרָאֵל
am'cha ahavta.	עַמְּךָ אָהָבְתָּ.
Torah umitzvot,	תּוֹרָה וּמִצְוֹת
chukim umishpatim	חֻקִּים וּמִשְׁפָּטִים
otanu limad'ta.	אוֹתָנוּ לִמַּדְתָּ.

God, You gave us the Torah
to show that You love us.
May it always be a friend at our side.

The Torah is our teacher.
It tells us what is right
and what is wrong.

It shows us how to live good lives.

Be with us always when we study Torah.

Be with us always,
as we try to live good lives.

Baruch ata, Adonai,	בָּרוּךְ אַתָּה, יְיָ,
oheiv amo Yisra-eil.	אוֹהֵב עַמּוֹ יִשְׂרָאֵל.

We praise You, Eternal God.
You gave the Jewish people the Torah.
It is your special gift to us.

◆◆

Sh'ma Yisra-eil:	שְׁמַע יִשְׂרָאֵל:
Adonai Eloheinu,	יהוה אֱלֹהֵינוּ,
Adonai echad!	יהוה אֶחָד!

Hear, O Israel: the Eternal One is our God, the Eternal God alone.

Baruch Sheim	בָּרוּךְ שֵׁם
k'vod malchuto	כְּבוֹד מַלְכוּתוֹ
l'olam va-ed!	לְעוֹלָם וָעֶד!

Blessed is God's glory forever and ever!

PLEASE BE SEATED

V'ahavta et	וְאָהַבְתָּ אֵת
Adonai Elohecha	יהוה אֱלֹהֶיךָ
b'chol l'vav'cha,	בְּכָל־לְבָבְךָ,
uv'chol nafsh'cha,	וּבְכָל־נַפְשְׁךָ,
uv'chol m'odecha.	וּבְכָל־מְאֹדֶךָ.

You shall love God in every way you can:

V'hayu had'varim	וְהָיוּ הַדְּבָרִים
ha-eileh asher	הָאֵלֶּה אֲשֶׁר
anochi m'tzav'cha	אָנֹכִי מְצַוְּךָ
hayom al l'vavecha.	הַיּוֹם עַל־לְבָבֶךָ.

Treat the Torah with respect.
Love its words.

V'shinantam l'vanecha.	וְשִׁנַּנְתָּם לְבָנֶיךָ.

Teach the Torah to your children.

V'dibarta bam	וְדִבַּרְתָּ בָּם
b'shivt'cha b'veitecha	בְּשִׁבְתְּךָ בְּבֵיתֶךָ
uv'lecht'cha vaderech.	וּבְלֶכְתְּךָ בַדֶּרֶךְ.

Talk about the Torah
at home and everywhere.
Make it an important part of your life.

Uv'shochb'cha	וּבְשָׁכְבְּךָ
uv'kumecha.	וּבְקוּמֶךָ.

Say the Sh'ma as you lie down to sleep
and as you rise up to begin a new day.

Uk'shartam l'ot	וּקְשַׁרְתָּם לְאוֹת
al yadecha,	עַל־יָדֶךָ,
v'hayu l'totafot	וְהָיוּ לְטֹטָפוֹת
bein einecha.	בֵּין עֵינֶיךָ.

Do what the
words in the Torah
say to do. Think
about them
wherever you are.

Uch'tavtam al m'zuzot	וּכְתַבְתָּם עַל־מְזוּזֹת
beitecha uvish'arecha.	בֵּיתֶךָ וּבִשְׁעָרֶיךָ.
L'ma-an tizk'ru	לְמַעַן תִּזְכְּרוּ
va-asitem	וַעֲשִׂיתֶם
et kol mitzvotai,	אֶת־כָּל־מִצְוֹתָי,
vih'yitem k'doshim	וִהְיִיתֶם קְדֹשִׁים
leiloheichem.	לֵאלֹהֵיכֶם.
Ani Adonai	אֲנִי יהוה
Eloheichem,	אֱלֹהֵיכֶם,
asher hotzeiti	אֲשֶׁר הוֹצֵאתִי
etchem	אֶתְכֶם
me-Eretz Mitzrayim	מֵאֶרֶץ מִצְרַיִם
lihyot lachem	לִהְיוֹת לָכֶם
leilohim.	לֵאלֹהִים.
Ani Adonai	אֲנִי יהוה
Eloheichem.	אֱלֹהֵיכֶם.

Put a mezuzah on your doorpost.
It reminds us to live by the wisdom
in the Torah.

Long ago,
our people were slaves to Pharaoh.

We prayed, "Dear God, help us to be free.
We don't want to be slaves any more."

Finally You sent Moses
to lead us out of Egypt.

He led us out,
so we could worship You in freedom.

When we came to the Sea,
the people sang a song
to thank You, God.

"Thank You," they sang,
"for setting us free."

When we sing it, we pray,
"Let everyone be free."

Mi chamocha	מִי־כָמֹכָה
ba-eilim, Adonai?	בָּאֵלִם, יהוה?
Mi kamocha,	מִי כָּמֹכָה,
ne-dar bakodesh,	נֶאְדָּר בַּקֹּדֶשׁ,
nora t'hilot,	נוֹרָא תְהִלֹּת,
osei feleh?	עֹשֵׂה פֶלֶא?

Malchut'cha	מַלְכוּתְךָ
ra-u vanecha,	רָאוּ בָנֶיךָ,
bokei-a yam	בּוֹקֵעַ יָם
lifnei Mosheh.	לִפְנֵי מֹשֶׁה.
Zeh Eili!	זֶה אֵלִי!
Anu v'am'ru:	עָנוּ וְאָמְרוּ:
Adonai yimloch	יהוה יִמְלֹךְ
l'olam va-ed.	לְעֹלָם וָעֶד!
V'ne-emar:	וְנֶאֱמַר:
ki fada Adonai	כִּי־פָדָה יהוה
et Ya-akov,	אֶת יַעֲקֹב,
ug'alo	וּגְאָלוֹ
miyad chazak	מִיַּד חָזָק
mimenu.	מִמֶּנּוּ.
Baruch ata, Adonai,	בָּרוּךְ אַתָּה, יי,
ga-al Yisra-eil.	גָּאַל יִשְׂרָאֵל.

We praise You, Eternal God.
You saved Your people, Israel.

Hashkiveinu,	הַשְׁכִּיבֵנוּ,
Adonai Eloheinu,	יי אֱלֹהֵינוּ,
l'shalom,	לְשָׁלוֹם,
v'ha-amideinu,	וְהַעֲמִידֵנוּ,
malkeinu, l'chayim.	מַלְכֵּנוּ, לְחַיִּים.

It is evening, and soon we will go to bed.

You are with us at all times, God,
when we sleep and when we wake.

When it is dark,
we turn to You for light.

When we are afraid,
we turn to You for courage.

When we feel weak,
we turn to You for strength.

Be with us tonight and always.
Help us to know You are there.

Baruch ata,	בָּרוּךְ אַתָּה,
Adonai, haporeis	יי, הַפּוֹרֵס
sukkat shalom aleinu.	סֻכַּת שָׁלוֹם עָלֵינוּ.

We praise You, Eternal God.
You help us feel safe and secure,
like being wrapped in a warm,
soft blanket.

◆◆

V'sham'ru	וְשָׁמְרוּ
v'nei Yisra-eil	בְנֵי־יִשְׂרָאֵל
et ha-Shabbat,	אֶת־הַשַּׁבָּת,
la-asot et ha-Shabbat	לַעֲשׂוֹת אֶת־הַשַּׁבָּת
l'dorotam	לְדֹרֹתָם
b'rit olam.	בְּרִית עוֹלָם.
Beini uvein	בֵּינִי וּבֵין
b'nei Yisra-eil,	בְּנֵי יִשְׂרָאֵל
ot hi l'olam.	אוֹת הִיא לְעֹלָם.
Ki sheishet yamim	כִּי שֵׁשֶׁת יָמִים
asa Adonai	עָשָׂה יהוה
et hashamayim	אֶת־הַשָּׁמַיִם
v'et ha-aretz,	וְאֶת־הָאָרֶץ,
uvayom hash'vi-i	וּבַיּוֹם הַשְּׁבִיעִי
shavat vayinafash.	שָׁבַת וַיִּנָּפַשׁ.

The children of Israel shall keep the Sabbath in every generation. It is a covenant for all time. For in six days God made the heavens and the earth. And on the seventh day God rested.

◆ SHABBAT IS HOLY ◆ קְדוּשַּׁת הַיּוֹם

God gave us Shabbat,
as a special, holy day.

When we celebrate Shabbat,
we make our lives holy.

We make our lives holy
when we rest.

We make our lives holy
when we pray.

We make our lives holy
when we study Torah.

We make our lives holy
when we share the joy of Shabbat.

Thank You, God, for this holy day.
Thank You, God, for Shabbat.

Baruch ata, Adonai,	בָּרוּךְ אַתָּה, יְיָ,
m'kadeish ha-Shabbat.	מְקַדֵּשׁ הַשַּׁבָּת.

We praise You, Eternal God:
You gave us Shabbat
to rest and pray and study.

◆ **PRAYERS OF ASKING** ◆

O God, You have made the world a special place. Help us make good things happen in the world.

You gave our people the Torah.

בָּרוּךְ אַתָּה, יי *Baruch ata, Adonai:*
Help us use Your book to learn wisdom.

You make healing possible.

בָּרוּךְ אַתָּה, יי *Baruch ata, Adonai:*
Help us heal those who are sick.

You show us how to learn
from our mistakes.

בָּרוּךְ אַתָּה, יי *Baruch ata, Adonai:*
Help us say, "I'm sorry,"
and "I forgive you."

You make the soil rich to grow food.

בָּרוּךְ אַתָּה, יי *Baruch ata, Adonai:*
Help us share with others.

You want people to be free.

בָּרוּךְ אַתָּה, יי *Baruch ata, Adonai:*
Help us work for everyone's freedom.

You taught us about justice.

בָּרוּךְ אַתָּה, יי *Baruch ata, Adonai:*
Help us always to be fair.

You love the Land of Israel
and the City of Jerusalem.

בָּרוּךְ אַתָּה, יי *Baruch ata, Adonai:*
Help us work for our Jewish homeland.

You are near to all who call on You.

בָּרוּךְ אַתָּה, יי *Baruch ata, Adonai:*
Help us know You are with us always.

Hear our prayers, God, and show us Your love. Help us always to know that You are everywhere. Here and at home, in the morning and at night, happy or sad, we turn to You. There is no God but You.

Baruch ata,	בָּרוּךְ אַתָּה,
Adonai, she-ot'cha	יי, שֶׁאוֹתְךָ
l'vad'cha b'yir-a	לְבַדְּךָ בְּיִרְאָה
na-avod.	נַעֲבוֹד.

We praise You, Eternal God.
We worship You, and You alone.

◆ THANKSGIVING / PEACE ◆
◆ הוֹדָאָה / בִּרְכַּת שָׁלוֹם ◆

We thank You, God, for Your many gifts.
When we think about these gifts,
we remember how blessed we are.

Thank You for giving us life.
Thank You for giving us a soul.
Thank You for always caring.

Baruch ata, Adonai,	בָּרוּךְ אַתָּה, יי,
osei hashalom.	עוֹשֵׂה הַשָּׁלוֹם.

We praise You, Eternal God.
You plant peace in our hearts
and in the world.

◆◆

SILENT PRAYER

All things bright and beautiful;
All things great and small;

All things wise and wonderful —
Dear God, You made them all.

Each lovely flower that opens;
Each little bird that sings —

You made their glowing colors;
You made their tiny wings.

The purple peaks of mountains;
The rivers flowing by;

The sunsets and the morning
That brighten up the sky;

The cold wind in the winter;
The pleasant summer sun;

The ripe fruits of the garden —
You made them every one.

You gave us eyes to see them
And lips that we might tell

How great are You, Almighty,
Who make all things well.

— OR —

You created the world, God.
We have many questions to ask
and many things to think about:

What causes the colors in a rainbow?
How does a snowflake form?
Why do people get sick?
Why do people have to die?
How do I know You are real?

Some questions are easy to answer.
Some are very difficult.

Help me understand Your universe, God.

The more pieces I can fit together,
the more I understand about You.

◆◆

Yihyu l'ratzon	יִהְיוּ לְרָצוֹן
imrei fi,	אִמְרֵי־פִי
v'hegyon libi	וְהֶגְיוֹן לִבִּי
l'fanecha,	לְפָנֶיךָ,
Adonai tzuri	יהוה צוּרִי
v'go-ali.	וְגוֹאֲלִי.

May the words of my mouth
and the meditations of my heart
be acceptable in Your sight, O God,
my Rock and my Redeemer.
Amen.

(For a Torah reading, turn to page 89.)
(For Closing Prayers, turn to page 99.)

For Shabbat or Weekdays

Evening Service II

I like to be with my friends:

Sometimes we laugh and sing together.

Sometimes we run and play together.

Sometimes we walk and talk together.

Sometimes we sit and eat together.

Sometimes we go to school
and learn together.

Today we have come to synagogue
to pray together.

Sh'ma and Its Blessings

שְׁמַע וּבִרְכוֹתֶיהָ

PLEASE RISE

Bar'chu et Adonai ham'vorach.	בָּרְכוּ אֶת־יי הַמְבֹרָךְ!
Baruch Adonai *ham'vorach* *l'olam va-ed.*	בָּרוּךְ יי הַמְבֹרָךְ לְעוֹלָם וָעֶד!

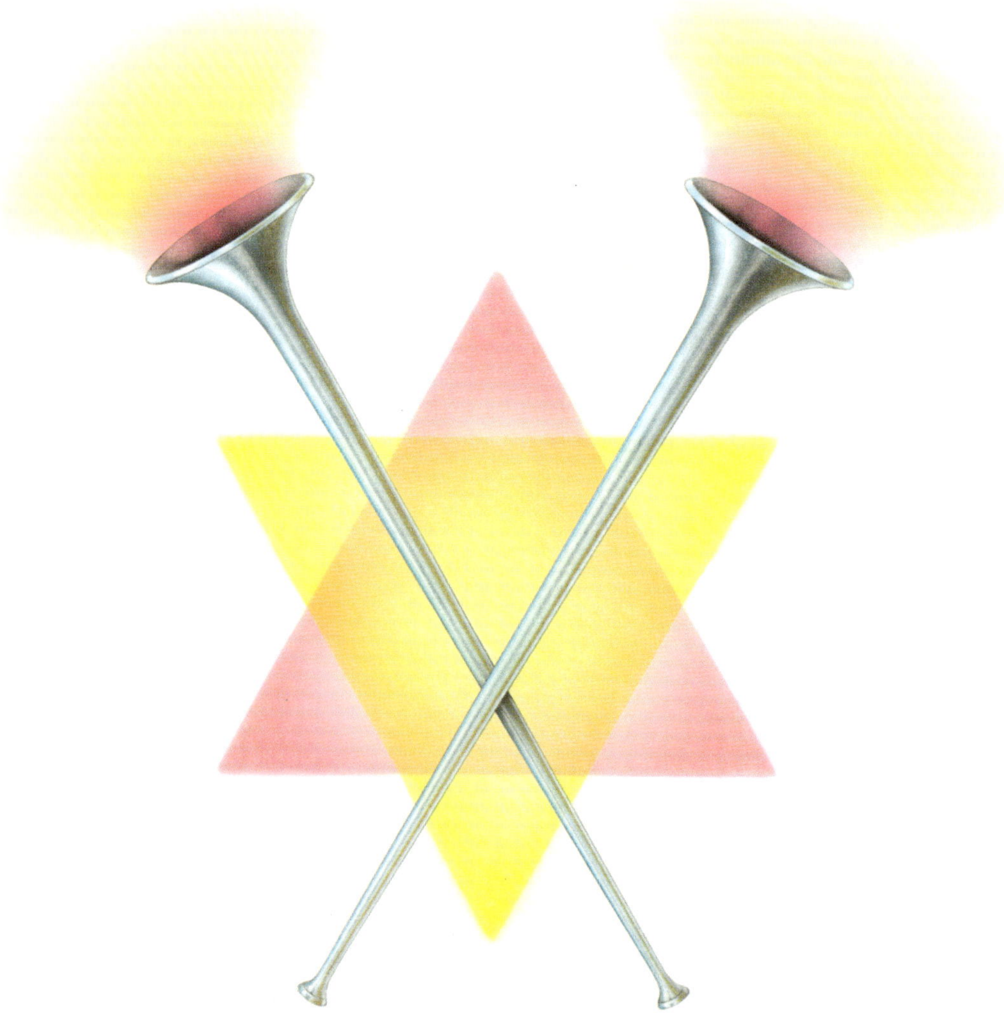

All things bright and beautiful;
All things great and small;
All things wise and wonderful —
Dear God, You made them all.

Each lovely flower that opens;
Each little bird that sings —
You made their glowing colors;
You made their tiny wings.

The purple peaks of mountains;
The rivers flowing by;
The sunsets and the morning
That brighten up the sky;

The cold wind in the winter;
The pleasant summer sun;
The ripe fruits of the garden —
You made them every one.

You gave us eyes to see them
And lips that we might tell
How great are You, Almighty,
Who make all things well.

Ahavat olam Beit Yisra-eil am'cha ahavta.	אַהֲבַת עוֹלָם בֵּית יִשְׂרָאֵל עַמְּךָ אָהָבְתָּ.

Long ago the Jewish people
discovered God's love.

They listened for God's word,
and wrote in the Torah what they heard:

Worship only God.

Don't make idols.

Don't break a promise.

Remember to celebrate Shabbat.

Honor your father and your mother.

Don't steal.

Don't be unfaithful
to your husband or wife.

Don't murder.

Don't be jealous of what other people have.

Don't tell lies.

Thank You, God, for these words.
When we read them, we know how to
live, and we remember that You love us.

Baruch ata, Adonai, oheiv amo Yisra-eil.	בָּרוּךְ אַתָּה, יְיָ, אוֹהֵב עַמּוֹ יִשְׂרָאֵל.

◆◆

Sh'ma Yisra-eil: שְׁמַע יִשְׂרָאֵל:
Adonai Eloheinu, יהוה אֱלֹהֵינוּ,
Adonai echad! יהוה אֶחָד!

Hear, O Israel: the Eternal One is our God, the Eternal God alone.

Baruch Sheim בָּרוּךְ שֵׁם
k'vod malchuto כְּבוֹד מַלְכוּתוֹ
l'olam va-ed! לְעוֹלָם וָעֶד!

Blessed is God's glory forever and ever!

PLEASE BE SEATED

V'ahavta et וְאָהַבְתָּ אֵת
Adonai Elohecha יהוה אֱלֹהֶיךָ
b'chol l'vav'cha, בְּכָל־לְבָבְךָ,
uv'chol nafsh'cha, וּבְכָל־נַפְשְׁךָ,
uv'chol m'odecha. וּבְכָל־מְאֹדֶךָ.
V'hayu had'varim וְהָיוּ הַדְּבָרִים
ha-eileh asher הָאֵלֶּה אֲשֶׁר
anochi m'tzav'cha אָנֹכִי מְצַוְּךָ
hayom al l'vavecha. הַיּוֹם עַל־לְבָבֶךָ.

V'shinantam l'vanecha	וְשִׁנַּנְתָּם לְבָנֶיךָ
v'dibarta bam	וְדִבַּרְתָּ בָּם
b'shivt'cha b'veitecha,	בְּשִׁבְתְּךָ בְּבֵיתֶךָ,
uv'lecht'cha vaderech,	וּבְלֶכְתְּךָ בַדֶּרֶךְ,
uv'shochb'cha	וּבְשָׁכְבְּךָ
uv'kumecha.	וּבְקוּמֶךָ.
Uk'shartam l'ot	וּקְשַׁרְתָּם לְאוֹת
al yadecha,	עַל־יָדֶךָ,
v'hayu l'totafot	וְהָיוּ לְטֹטָפוֹת
bein einecha.	בֵּין עֵינֶיךָ.
Uch'tavtam al m'zuzot	וּכְתַבְתָּם עַל־מְזוּזֹת
beitecha uvish'arecha.	בֵּיתֶךָ וּבִשְׁעָרֶיךָ.

L'ma-an tizk'ru	לְמַעַן תִּזְכְּרוּ
va-asitem	וַעֲשִׂיתֶם
et kol mitzvotai,	אֶת־כָּל־מִצְוֹתָי,
vih'yitem k'doshim	וִהְיִיתֶם קְדֹשִׁים
leiloheichem.	לֵאלֹהֵיכֶם.
Ani Adonai	אֲנִי יהוה
Eloheichem,	אֱלֹהֵיכֶם,
asher hotzeiti	אֲשֶׁר הוֹצֵאתִי
etchem	אֶתְכֶם
me-Eretz Mitzrayim	מֵאֶרֶץ מִצְרַיִם
lihyot lachem	לִהְיוֹת לָכֶם
leilohim.	לֵאלֹהִים.
Ani Adonai	אֲנִי יהוה
Eloheichem.	אֱלֹהֵיכֶם.

You shall love God in every way you can.

Treat the Torah with love and respect.

Teach the Torah to your children
when you grow up.

Talk about the Torah at home
and everywhere.

Say the Sh'ma when you lie down
and when you rise up.

Place a mezuzah on your doorpost.

Do what the words in the Torah
say to do.

Think about the words in the Torah
wherever you are,
whatever you are doing.

Remember to follow the ways of Torah.
Try to be holy like God.

Long ago, the Jewish people
were slaves in Egypt.

You sent Moses to help our ancestors, so they could go free to worship You. They sang a song to thank You:

Mi chamocha	מִי־כָמֹכָה
ba-eilim, Adonai?	בָּאֵלִם, יהוה?

Who is like You, God of the universe?

Still today there are people who are not free. We pray that they will be set free.

Then all who worship You
will sing for joy:

Mi chamocha	מִי־כָמֹכָה
ba-eilim, Adonai?	בָּאֵלִם, יהוה?
Mi kamocha,	מִי כָּמֹכָה,
ne'dar bakodesh,	נֶאְדָּר בַּקֹּדֶשׁ,
nora t'hilot,	נוֹרָא תְהִלֹּת,
osei feleh?	עֹשֵׂה פֶלֶא?
Malchut'cha	מַלְכוּתְךָ
ra-u vanecha,	רָאוּ בָנֶיךָ,
bokei-a yam	בּוֹקֵעַ יָם
lifnei Mosheh.	לִפְנֵי מֹשֶׁה.
Zeh Eli!	זֶה אֵלִי!
Anu v'am'ru:	עָנוּ וְאָמְרוּ:
Adonai yimloch	יהוה יִמְלֹךְ
l'olam va-ed!	לְעֹלָם וָעֶד!

Baruch ata, Adonai,	בָּרוּךְ אַתָּה, יי,
ga-al Yisra-eil.	גָּאַל יִשְׂרָאֵל.

We praise You, Eternal God.
You freed the Jewish people from slavery.

Help us go to sleep in peace, O God,
and to wake up in the morning
feeling good.

Guard us from harm outside our houses
and inside them.
Like a mother bird protects her young
with her covering wing,
please protect us.

Baruch ata, Adonai,	בָּרוּךְ אַתָּה, יְיָ,
shomeir amo	שׁוֹמֵר עַמּוֹ
Yisra-eil la-ad.	יִשְׂרָאֵל לָעַד.

We praise You, Eternal God.
You always guard
Your people Israel.

◆◆

V'sham'ru	וְשָׁמְרוּ
v'nei Yisra-eil	בְנֵי־יִשְׂרָאֵל
et ha-Shabbat,	אֶת־הַשַּׁבָּת,
la-asot et ha-Shabbat	לַעֲשׂוֹת אֶת־הַשַּׁבָּת
l'dorotam	לְדֹרֹתָם
b'rit olam.	בְּרִית עוֹלָם.
Beini uvein	בֵּינִי וּבֵין
b'nei Yisra-eil,	בְּנֵי יִשְׂרָאֵל
ot hi l'olam.	אוֹת הִיא לְעֹלָם.
Ki sheishet yamim	כִּי שֵׁשֶׁת יָמִים
asa Adonai	עָשָׂה יהוה
et hashamayim	אֶת־הַשָּׁמַיִם
v'et ha-aretz,	וְאֶת־הָאָרֶץ,
uvayom hash'vi-i	וּבַיּוֹם הַשְּׁבִיעִי
shavat vayinafash.	שָׁבַת וַיִּנָּפַשׁ.

The children of Israel shall keep the Sabbath in every generation. It is a covenant for all time. For in six days God made the heavens and the earth. And on the seventh day God rested.

T'filah

תְּפִלָּה

PLEASE RISE

◆ אָבוֹת וְאִמָּהוֹת / גְּבוּרוֹת / קְדוּשָּׁה ◆

Baruch ata, Adonai,	בָּרוּךְ אַתָּה, יי,
Eloheinu veilohei	אֱלֹהֵינוּ וֵאלֹהֵי
avoteinu v'imoteinu:	אֲבוֹתֵינוּ וְאִמּוֹתֵינוּ:
Elohei Avraham,	אֱלֹהֵי אַבְרָהָם,
Elohei Yitzchak,	אֱלֹהֵי יִצְחָק,
veilohei Ya-akov.	וֵאלֹהֵי יַעֲקֹב.
Elohei Sara,	אֱלֹהֵי שָׂרָה,
Elohei Rivka,	אֱלֹהֵי רִבְקָה,
Elohei Lei-a,	אֱלֹהֵי לֵאָה,
veilohei Racheil.	וֵאלֹהֵי רָחֵל.
Ha-eil hagadol	הָאֵל הַגָּדוֹל
hagibor v'hanora,	הַגִּבּוֹר וְהַנּוֹרָא,
eil elyon,	אֵל עֶלְיוֹן,
gomeil	גּוֹמֵל
chasadim tovim	חֲסָדִים טוֹבִים
v'konei hakol,	וְקוֹנֵה הַכֹּל,
v'zocheir chasdei	וְזוֹכֵר חַסְדֵי
avot v'imahot,	אָבוֹת וְאִמָּהוֹת,
umeivi g'ula	וּמֵבִיא גְּאֻלָּה
liv'nei v'neihem,	לִבְנֵי בְנֵיהֶם,
l'ma-an sh'mo	לְמַעַן שְׁמוֹ
b'ahava.	בְּאַהֲבָה.

Melech ozeir	מֶלֶךְ עוֹזֵר
umoshi-a umagein.	וּמוֹשִׁיעַ וּמָגֵן.
Baruch ata, Adonai,	בָּרוּךְ אַתָּה, יי,
magein Avraham	מָגֵן אַבְרָהָם
v'ezrat Sara.	וְעֶזְרַת שָׂרָה.

We praise You, *We praise You,*
Eternal God: *Eternal God:*
God of Abraham, *God of Sarah,*
God of Isaac, *God of Rebekah,*
God of Jacob, *Leah and Rachel,*
God of all generations.

You are powerful, God,
and You can do anything.

*You help us feel safe when we are afraid,
and make us feel better when we are sick.*

Blessed is our God,
Shield of Abraham and Sarah.

*Blessed is our God,
Creator of Life.*

God, everywhere we turn
we feel Your power and Your holiness.

We feel You with us
when we hear a newborn baby cry.

Kadosh, kadosh, קָדוֹשׁ, קָדוֹשׁ,
kadosh. קָדוֹשׁ.

We feel You with us
when we touch a soft flower.

Holy, holy, holy.

We feel You with us
when we see a rainbow after a storm.

Kadosh, kadosh, קָדוֹשׁ, קָדוֹשׁ,
kadosh. קָדוֹשׁ.

We feel You with us
when we are loving and loved.

Holy, holy, holy.

We feel You with us
when we do a mitzvah.

Kadosh, kadosh,	קָדוֹשׁ, קָדוֹשׁ,
kadosh.	קָדוֹשׁ.
Baruch ata, Adonai,	בָּרוּךְ אַתָּה, יי,
ha-Eil hakadosh.	הָאֵל הַקָּדוֹשׁ.

We praise You, Eternal God.
Everywhere we turn, You are there.

PLEASE BE SEATED

◆ PRECIOUS DAY ◆

Thank You, God, for Shabbat.
It is an important day. It is a holy day.

On Shabbat we remember
You created the world.

On Shabbat we remember to be holy.

On Shabbat we feel close to You.

On Shabbat we feel close to our family.

May our lives be blessed on this Shabbat
and every Shabbat.

Baruch ata,	בָּרוּךְ אַתָּה,
Adonai, m'kadeish	יי, מְקַדֵּשׁ
ha-Shabbat.	הַשַּׁבָּת.

We praise You, Eternal God.
You make Shabbat holy.

Yism'chu	יִשְׂמְחוּ
v'malchut'cha	בְמַלְכוּתְךָ
shom'rei Shabbat	שׁוֹמְרֵי שַׁבָּת
v'kor'ei oneg.	וְקוֹרְאֵי עֹנֶג.
Am m'kad'shei	עַם מְקַדְּשֵׁי
sh'vi-i, kulam	שְׁבִיעִי, כֻּלָּם
yisb'u v'yit-an'gu	יִשְׂבְּעוּ וְיִתְעַנְּגוּ
mituvecha.	מִטּוּבֶךָ.

V'hash'vi-i	וְהַשְּׁבִיעִי
ratzita bo	רָצִיתָ בּוֹ
v'kidashto.	וְקִדַּשְׁתּוֹ.
Chemdat yamim	חֶמְדַּת יָמִים
oto karata,	אוֹתוֹ קָרָֽאתָ,
zeicher l'ma-asei	זֵֽכֶר לְמַֽעֲשֵׂה
v'reishit.	בְרֵאשִׁית.

FOR WEEKDAYS

◆ PRAYERS OF ASKING ◆

We thank You, God,
for minds that think.

And we pray to use them well.

We thank You for helping us
do what is right.

And we pray to know right from wrong.

We thank You, God, for hands that heal.

And we pray that our bodies be strong.

We thank You for letting us
talk with You.

And we pray that you will always
hear our prayer.

◆◆

We pray for peace.

Peace for everyone, everywhere.

Peace for soldiers fighting wars.

Peace for people who live
where soldiers are fighting around them.

Peace for parents who are worried
about their children.

Peace for children who are worried
about their parents.

Peace for people who are struggling
with others.

Peace for people who are stuggling
with themselves.

Baruch ata, Adonai,	בָּרוּךְ אַתָּה, יְיָ,
osei hashalom.	עוֹשֵׂה הַשָּׁלוֹם.

We praise You, Eternal God.
You help us make peace.
And you help us find peace.

◆

Sim shalom,	שִׂים שָׁלוֹם,
tova uv'racha.	טוֹבָה וּבְרָכָה.

— OR —

Shalom rav	שָׁלוֹם רָב
al Yisra-eil	עַל יִשְׂרָאֵל
am'cha	עַמְּךָ
tasim l'olam,	תָּשִׂים לְעוֹלָם,
ki ata hu	כִּי אַתָּה הוּא
melech adon	מֶלֶךְ אָדוֹן
l'chol hashalom.	לְכָל־הַשָּׁלוֹם.
V'tov b'einecha	וְטוֹב בְּעֵינֶיךָ
l'vareich et	לְבָרֵךְ אֶת־
am'cha Yisra-eil	עַמְּךָ יִשְׂרָאֵל
b'chol eit	בְּכָל־עֵת
uv'chol sha-a	וּבְכָל־שָׁעָה
bish'lomecha.	בִּשְׁלוֹמֶךָ.

◆◆

Dear God: It is wonderful to be alive.
I have been given many blessings:
food to eat, clothes to wear,
people who love me.
Thank You, God,
for all of my wonderful blessings.

◆◆

Yihyu l'ratzon	יִהְיוּ לְרָצוֹן
imrei fi,	אִמְרֵי־פִי
v'hegyon libi	וְהֶגְיוֹן לִבִּי
l'fanecha,	לְפָנֶיךָ,
Adonai, tzuri v'go-ali.	יהוה, צוּרִי וְגוֹאֲלִי.

May the words of my mouth
and the thoughts in my heart
be pleasing to You, O God.

(For a Torah reading, turn to page 89.)
(For Closing Prayers, turn to page 99.)

For Shabbat or Weekdays

Morning Service I

Morning Blessings

בִּרְכוֹת הַשַּׁחַר

מַה־טֹּבוּ
אֹהָלֶיךָ, יַעֲקֹב,
מִשְׁכְּנֹתֶיךָ,
יִשְׂרָאֵל!

Ma tovu
ohalecha, Ya-akov,
mishk'notecha,
Yisra-eil!

How lovely are your tents, O Jacob,
your dwelling places, O Israel!

Thank You, God,
for eyes that see,

for ears that hear,
for lips that speak.

Thank you, God,
for minds that think.

Thank You, God,
for hearts that beat.

Baruch ata, Adonai,	בָּרוּךְ אַתָּה, יי,
asher yatzar	אֲשֶׁר יָצַר
et ha-adam	אֶת־הָאָדָם
b'chochma.	בְּחָכְמָה.

We praise You, Eternal God.
Thank You for my body.
It is a miracle!

Sh'ma and Its Blessings

שְׁמַע וּבִרְכוֹתֶיהָ

PLEASE RISE

Bar'chu et Adonai ham'vorach.	בָּרְכוּ אֶת־יי הַמְבֹרָךְ!
Baruch Adonai *ham'vorach* *l'olam va-ed.*	בָּרוּךְ יי הַמְבֹרָךְ לְעוֹלָם וָעֶד!

When God made the world,
God made it full of light;
the sun to shine by day,
the moon and stars by night.
God made it full of life:
lilies, oaks, and trout,
tigers and bears,
sparrows, hawks, and apes.

Then God took clay
from earth's four corners
to give it the breath of life.
And God said: This is very good!

Man, woman, and child —
all are good;
man, woman, child resemble God.

Like God, we love.
Like God, we think.
Like God, we care.

Man, woman, and child —
all are good.

God, You gave us mitzvot in the Torah because You love us:

Play fair.

Be kind.

Share with others.

Tell the truth.

When we want to know the right thing to do, we remember what the Torah says. It helps us decide what is right, when no one is there to tell us.

Baruch ata, Adonai,	בָּרוּךְ אַתָּה, יְיָ,
oheiv amo Yisra-eil.	אוֹהֵב עַמּוֹ יִשְׂרָאֵל.

We praise You, Eternal God.
You gave the Jewish people the Torah.
It is a sign that You love us.

◆◆

Sh'ma Yisra-eil:	שְׁמַע יִשְׂרָאֵל:
Adonai Eloheinu,	יהוה אֱלֹהֵינוּ,
Adonai echad!	יהוה אֶחָד!

Hear, O Israel: the Eternal One is our God, the Eternal God alone.

Baruch Sheim	בָּרוּךְ שֵׁם
k'vod malchuto	כְּבוֹד מַלְכוּתוֹ
l'olam va-ed!	לְעוֹלָם וָעֶד!

Blessed is God's glory forever and ever!

PLEASE BE SEATED

Our ancestors wrote in the Torah,
"וְאָהַבְתָּ אֵת יהוה אֱלֹהֶיךָ V'ahavta et
Adonai Elohecha — You shall love God."

We show our love for God
when parents and teachers share Torah
with their children.

We show our love for God
when we study the words of Torah.

We show our love for God
when we say the Sh'ma
each night and day.

We show our love for God
when we put a mezuzah
on our doorpost.

We show our love for God
when we do what the Torah says,
even when no one is there to remind us.

The Torah tells us the Jewish people
were slaves in Egypt.

We prayed, "Dear God, help us be free.
We don't want to be slaves to Pharaoh."

You sent Moses to lead us out of Egypt.

Moses led us out,
so we could worship You in freedom.

When we came to the sea,
the people sang a song to thank You, God.

We still sing the same song.
When we sing it, we pray,
"Let everyone be free.

Free from cruel rulers
and free from idols.

Free to believe and think for themselves."

Mi chamocha	מִי־כָמֹכָה
ba-eilim, Adonai?	בָּאֵלִם, יהוה?
Mi kamocha,	מִי כָּמֹכָה,
ne-dar bakodesh,	נֶאְדָּר בַּקֹּדֶשׁ,
nora t'hilot,	נוֹרָא תְהִלֹּת,
osei feleh?	עֹשֵׂה פֶלֶא?

Shira chadasha	שִׁירָה חֲדָשָׁה
shib'chu g'ulim	שִׁבְּחוּ גְאוּלִים
l'shimcha al	לְשִׁמְךָ עַל־
s'fat hayam;	שְׂפַת הַיָּם;
yachad kulam hodu	יַחַד כֻּלָּם הוֹדוּ
v'himlichu v'amru:	וְהִמְלִיכוּ וְאָמְרוּ:
Adonai yimloch	יהוה יִמְלֹךְ
l'olam va-ed!	לְעוֹלָם וָעֶד!

Tzur Yisra-eil,	צוּר יִשְׂרָאֵל,
kuma	קוּמָה
b'ezrat Yisra-eil,	בְּעֶזְרַת יִשְׂרָאֵל,
uf'dei chin'umecha	וּפְדֵה כִנְאֻמֶךָ
Yehuda v'Yisra-eil.	יְהוּדָה וְיִשְׂרָאֵל.
Go-aleinu, Adonai	גֹּאֲלֵנוּ, יי
Tz'va-ot sh'mo,	צְבָאוֹת שְׁמוֹ,
K'dosh Yisra-eil.	קְדוֹשׁ יִשְׂרָאֵל.
Baruch ata, Adonai,	בָּרוּךְ אַתָּה, יי,
ga-al Yisra-eil.	גָּאַל יִשְׂרָאֵל.

We praise You, Eternal God.
You saved Your people Israel.

T'filah

תְּפִלָּה

PLEASE RISE

◆ **GOD OF ALL GENERATIONS** ◆ אָבוֹת וְאִמָּהוֹת

Baruch ata, Adonai,	בָּרוּךְ אַתָּה, יי,

We praise You, Eternal God,

Eloheinu veilohei	אֱלֹהֵינוּ וֵאלֹהֵי
avoteinu v'imoteinu:	אֲבוֹתֵינוּ וְאִמּוֹתֵינוּ:

Our God and God of our ancestors:

Elohei	אֱלֹהֵי
Avraham v'Sara,	אַבְרָהָם וְשָׂרָה,

God of Abraham and Sarah,

Elohei	אֱלֹהֵי
Yitzchak v'Rivka,	יִצְחָק וְרִבְקָה,

God of Isaac and Rebekah,

veilohei Ya'akov,	וֵאלֹהֵי יַעֲקֹב,
Lei-a v'Rachel.	לֵאָה וְרָחֵל.

God of Jacob, Leah and Rachel .

Baruch ata, Adonai,	בָּרוּךְ אַתָּה, יי,
magein Avraham	מָגֵן אַבְרָהָם
v'ezrat Sara.	וְעֶזְרַת שָׂרָה.

We praise You, Eternal God. Always be a shield, and protect the Jewish people.

You are holy, God.
We want to be like You.

You are strong.
We want to be strong.

You help people in trouble.
We want to help people in trouble.

You make freedom possible.
We want to make freedom possible.

You taught the Jews who came before us
how to live good lives.
We want to live good lives.

You are holy, God.
We want to be holy too.

◆

N'kadesh et shimcha	נְקַדֵּשׁ אֶת־שִׁמְךָ
ba-olam, k'shem	בָּעוֹלָם, כְּשֵׁם
shemakdishim	שֶׁמַּקְדִּישִׁים
oto bish'mei marom,	אוֹתוֹ בִּשְׁמֵי מָרוֹם,
kakatuv al yad	כַּכָּתוּב עַל־יַד
n'vi-echa: v'kara	נְבִיאֶךָ: וְקָרָא
zeh el zeh v'amar:	זֶה אֶל־זֶה וְאָמַר:

קָדוֹשׁ, קָדוֹשׁ,
קָדוֹשׁ יהוה
צְבָאוֹת, מְלֹא
כׇל־הָאָרֶץ
כְּבוֹדוֹ.

Kadosh, kadosh,
kadosh Adonai
Tz'va-ot, m'lo
chol ha-aretz
k'vodo.

אַדִּיר אַדִּירֵנוּ,
יהוה אֲדֹנֵינוּ,
מָה־אַדִּיר שִׁמְךָ
בְּכׇל־הָאָרֶץ!

Adir adireinu,
Adonai adoneinu,
ma adir shimcha
b'chol ha-aretz.

בָּרוּךְ כְּבוֹד־
יהוה מִמְּקוֹמוֹ.

Baruch k'vod
Adonai mim'komo.

Echad hu Eloheinu,	אֶחָד הוּא אֱלֹהֵינוּ,
Hu avinu,	הוּא אָבִינוּ,
hu malkeinu,	הוּא מַלְכֵּנוּ,
hu moshi-einu;	הוּא מוֹשִׁיעֵנוּ;
v'hu yashmi-einu	וְהוּא יַשְׁמִיעֵנוּ
b'rachamav	בְּרַחֲמָיו
l'einei kol chai:	לְעֵינֵי כָּל־חָי:
Ani Adonai	אֲנִי יהוה
Eloheichem!	אֱלֹהֵיכֶם!
Yimloch Adonai	יִמְלֹךְ יהוה
l'olam, Elohayich	לְעוֹלָם, אֱלֹהַיִךְ
Tziyon, l'dor vador.	צִיּוֹן, לְדֹר וָדֹר.
Halleluyah!	הַלְלוּיָהּ!
Baruch ata, Adonai,	בָּרוּךְ אַתָּה, יי,
ha-Eil hakadosh.	הָאֵל הַקָּדוֹשׁ.

We praise You, Eternal God.
You are holy.

PLEASE BE SEATED

We thank You, God,
for the gift of Shabbat.

Shabbat is a time
to rest with friends and family.

Shabbat is a time
to study and pray.

Shabbat is a time
to think about our blessings.

When we rest and pray,
study and remember our blessings,
we make our lives more holy.

Baruch ata,	בָּרוּךְ אַתָּה,
Adonai, m'kadeish	יי, מְקַדֵּשׁ
ha-Shabbat.	הַשַּׁבָּת.

We praise You, Eternal God,
for the holy Sabbath day.

Yism'chu	יִשְׂמְחוּ
v'malchut'cha	בְמַלְכוּתְךָ
shom'rei Shabbat	שׁוֹמְרֵי שַׁבָּת
v'kor'ei oneg.	וְקוֹרְאֵי עֹנֶג.
Am m'kad'shei	עַם מְקַדְּשֵׁי
sh'vi-i, kulam	שְׁבִיעִי, כֻּלָּם
yisb'u v'yit-an'gu	יִשְׂבְּעוּ וְיִתְעַנְּגוּ
mituvecha.	מִטּוּבֶךָ.

V'hash'vi-i	וְהַשְּׁבִיעִי
ratzita bo	רָצִיתָ בּוֹ
v'kidashto.	וְקִדַּשְׁתּוֹ.
Chemdat yamim	חֶמְדַּת יָמִים
oto karata,	אוֹתוֹ קָרָאתָ,
zeicher l'ma-asei	זֵכֶר לְמַעֲשֵׂה
v'reishit.	בְרֵאשִׁית.

FOR WEEKDAYS

◆ PRAYERS OF ASKING ◆

We thank You, God,
for minds that think.

And we pray to use them well.

We thank You for helping us
do what is right.

And we pray to know right from wrong.

We thank You, God, for hands that heal.

And we pray that our bodies be strong.

We thank You for letting us
talk with You.

And we pray that you will always
hear our prayer.

◆◆

Sim shalom,
tova uv'racha,
chein vachesed
v'rachamim,
aleinu v'al kol
Yisra-eil amecha.

שִׂים שָׁלוֹם,
טוֹבָה וּבְרָכָה,
חֵן וָחֶסֶד
וְרַחֲמִים,
עָלֵינוּ וְעַל כָּל־
יִשְׂרָאֵל עַמֶּךָ.

בָּרְכֵנוּ אָבִינוּ,	*Bar'cheinu avinu,*
כֻּלָּנוּ כְּאֶחָד,	*kulanu k'echad,*
בְּאוֹר פָּנֶיךָ,	*b'or panecha,*
כִּי בְאוֹר פָּנֶיךָ	*ki v'or panecha*
נָתַתָּ לָּנוּ,	*natata lanu,*
יי אֱלֹהֵינוּ,	*Adonai Eloheinu,*
תּוֹרַת חַיִּים	*torat chayim*
וְאַהֲבַת חֶסֶד,	*v'ahavat chesed,*
וּצְדָקָה וּבְרָכָה	*utz'daka uv'racha*
וְרַחֲמִים, וְחַיִּים	*v'rachamim, v'chayim*
וְשָׁלוֹם.	*v'shalom.*

וְטוֹב בְּעֵינֶיךָ	*V'tov b'einecha*
לְבָרֵךְ אֶת־	*l'vareich et*
עַמְּךָ יִשְׂרָאֵל	*am'cha Yisra-eil*
בְּכָל־עֵת	*b'chol eit*
וּבְכָל־שָׁעָה	*uv'chol sha-a*
בִּשְׁלוֹמֶךָ.	*bish'lomecha.*
בָּרוּךְ אַתָּה,	*Baruch ata,*
יי, הַמְבָרֵךְ	*Adonai, ham'vareich*
אֶת־עַמּוֹ יִשְׂרָאֵל	*et amo Yisra-eil*
בַּשָּׁלוֹם.	*bashalom.*

We praise You, God. You bless Your people Israel with peace.

Growing is important, God.

As I grow, I can reach more things.

As I grow, I can do more.

As I grow, I can understand more ideas.

As I grow, I can become a better person.

Help me grow, God.

I want to reach more,
do more, understand more,
and become a better person.

◆◆

Yihyu l'ratzon	יִהְיוּ לְרָצוֹן
imrei fi,	אִמְרֵי־פִי
v'hegyon libi	וְהֶגְיוֹן לִבִּי
l'fanecha, Adonai,	לְפָנֶיךָ, יהוה,
tzuri v'go-ali.	צוּרִי וְגוֹאֲלִי.

May the words of my mouth
and the thoughts in my heart
be pleasing to You, O God.

(For a Torah reading, turn to page 89.)

(For Closing Prayers, turn to page 99.)

For Shabbat or Weekdays

Morning Service II

Prayer is the way we speak to God.

Sometimes we pray alone,

sometimes we pray with others.

Sometimes we pray out loud,

sometimes we pray silently.

Sometimes we pray with our words,

sometimes we pray with our deeds.

Sometimes we say our prayers,

sometimes we sing them.

Sometimes we pray in English,

sometimes we pray in Hebrew.

However we pray, God,

we pray You will always hear us.

Sh'ma and Its Blessings

שְׁמַע וּבִרְכוֹתֶיהָ

PLEASE RISE

Bar'chu et Adonai	בָּרְכוּ אֶת־יי
ham'vorach.	הַמְבֹרָךְ!
Baruch Adonai	בָּרוּךְ יי
ham'vorach	הַמְבֹרָךְ
l'olam va-ed.	לְעוֹלָם וָעֶד!

◆ **CREATION** ◆ יוֹצֵר

Baruch ata, Adonai,	בָּרוּךְ אַתָּה, יי,
Eloheinu, melech	אֱלֹהֵינוּ, מֶלֶךְ
ha-olam, yotzeir	הָעוֹלָם, יוֹצֵר
or uvorei choshech,	אוֹר וּבוֹרֵא חֹשֶׁךְ,
oseh shalom	עֹשֶׂה שָׁלוֹם
uvorei et hakol.	וּבוֹרֵא אֶת־הַכֹּל.

Thank You, God, for creating the world.
It is filled with wonderful things:

Green grass and blue skies.
The warm sun and the starry night,
White clouds and gray clouds,
And flowers of every color.
Giant mountains and tiny ants,
Wide oceans and narrow streams.

בָּרוּךְ אַתָּה, יי,
יוֹצֵר הַמְּאוֹרוֹת.

Baruch ata, Adonai,
yotzeir ham'orot.

Thank You, God, for light,
so we can see them all.

God, the Torah is filled with Your love.
Its words teach us how to live:

You shall have no God except Me.

Do not make idols.

Do not make promises
you don't mean to keep.

Remember to celebrate Shabbat.

Honor your father and your mother.

Do not steal.

Do not be unfaithful
to your husband or your wife.

Do not murder.

Do not be jealous
of what other people have.

Do not tell lies.

We show our love for You, God,
by trying to follow Your words.

Baruch ata, Adonai,	בָּרוּךְ אַתָּה, יְיָ,
oheiv amo Yisra-eil.	אוֹהֵב עַמּוֹ יִשְׂרָאֵל.

We praise You, Eternal God,
for the Torah which shines
with Your love.

◆◆

Sh'ma Yisra-eil:
Adonai Eloheinu,
Adonai echad!

שְׁמַע יִשְׂרָאֵל:
יהוה אֱלֹהֵינוּ,
יהוה אֶחָד!

Hear, O Israel: the Eternal One is our God, the Eternal God alone.

Baruch Sheim
k'vod malchuto
l'olam va-ed!

בָּרוּךְ שֵׁם
כְּבוֹד מַלְכוּתוֹ
לְעוֹלָם וָעֶד!

Blessed is God's glory forever and ever!

PLEASE BE SEATED

V'ahavta et
Adonai Elohecha
b'chol l'vav'cha,
uv'chol nafsh'cha,
uv'chol m'odecha.

וְאָהַבְתָּ אֵת
יהוה אֱלֹהֶיךָ
בְּכָל־לְבָבְךָ,
וּבְכָל־נַפְשְׁךָ,
וּבְכָל־מְאֹדֶךָ.

You shall love God in every way you can:

V'hayu had'varim
ha-eileh asher
anochi m'tzav'cha
hayom al l'vavecha.

וְהָיוּ הַדְּבָרִים
הָאֵלֶּה אֲשֶׁר
אָנֹכִי מְצַוְּךָ
הַיּוֹם עַל־לְבָבֶךָ.

Treat the Torah with respect.
Love its words.

V'shinantam l'vanecha.	וְשִׁנַּנְתָּם לְבָנֶיךָ.

Teach the Torah to your children.

V'dibarta bam	וְדִבַּרְתָּ בָּם
b'shivt'cha b'veitecha	בְּשִׁבְתְּךָ בְּבֵיתֶךָ
uv'lecht'cha vaderech.	וּבְלֶכְתְּךָ בַדֶּרֶךְ.

Talk about the Torah
at home and everywhere.
Make it an important part of your life.

Uv'shochb'cha	וּבְשָׁכְבְּךָ
uv'kumecha.	וּבְקוּמֶךָ.

Say the Sh'ma as you lie down to sleep
and as you rise up to begin a new day.

Uk'shartam l'ot	וּקְשַׁרְתָּם לְאוֹת
al yadecha,	עַל־יָדֶךָ,
v'hayu l'totafot	וְהָיוּ לְטֹטָפוֹת
bein einecha.	בֵּין עֵינֶיךָ.

Do what the words in the Torah say to do.
Think about them wherever you are.

Uch'tavtam al m'zuzot	וּכְתַבְתָּם עַל־מְזוּזֹת
beitecha uvish'arecha.	בֵּיתֶךָ וּבִשְׁעָרֶיךָ.
L'ma-an tizk'ru	לְמַעַן תִּזְכְּרוּ
va-asitem	וַעֲשִׂיתֶם
et kol mitzvotai,	אֶת־כָּל־מִצְוֹתָי,
vih'yitem k'doshim	וִהְיִיתֶם קְדֹשִׁים
leiloheichem.	לֵאלֹהֵיכֶם.
Ani Adonai	אֲנִי יהוה
Eloheichem,	אֱלֹהֵיכֶם,
asher hotzeiti	אֲשֶׁר הוֹצֵאתִי
etchem	אֶתְכֶם
me-Eretz Mitzrayim	מֵאֶרֶץ מִצְרַיִם
lihyot lachem	לִהְיוֹת לָכֶם
leilohim.	לֵאלֹהִים.
Ani Adonai	אֲנִי יהוה
Eloheichem.	אֱלֹהֵיכֶם.

Put a mezuzah on your doorpost.
Touch it to remind you to live
by the wisdom in the Torah.

Long ago the Jewish people were slaves to Pharaoh in Egypt. They prayed to You for help. You sent Moses to help them so they could worship You in freedom.

Some people still are not free from slavery. Help us to help them. Then everyone can sing this song and love You in freedom:

מִי־כָמֹכָה
בָּאֵלִם, יהוה?
מִי כָּמֹכָה,
נֶאְדָּר בַּקֹּדֶשׁ,
נוֹרָא תְהִלֹּת,
עֹשֵׂה פֶלֶא?

Mi chamocha
ba-eilim, Adonai?
Mi kamocha,
ne-dar bakodesh,
nora t'hilot,
osei feleh?

שִׁירָה חֲדָשָׁה
שִׁבְּחוּ גְאוּלִים
לְשִׁמְךָ
עַל־שְׂפַת הַיָּם;
יַחַד כֻּלָּם הוֹדוּ
וְהִמְלִיכוּ וְאָמְרוּ:

Shira chadasha
shib'chu g'ulim
l'shimcha
al s'fat hayam;
yachad kulam hodu
v'himlichu v'amru:

יהוה יִמְלֹךְ
לְעוֹלָם וָעֶד!

Adonai yimloch
l'olam va-ed!

צוּר יִשְׂרָאֵל, קוּמָה
בְּעֶזְרַת יִשְׂרָאֵל,
וּפְדֵה כִנְאֻמֶךָ
יְהוּדָה וְיִשְׂרָאֵל.
גֹּאֲלֵנוּ, יי
צְבָאוֹת שְׁמוֹ,
קְדוֹשׁ יִשְׂרָאֵל.

Tzur Yisra-eil, kuma
b'ezrat Yisra-eil,
uf'dei chin'umecha
Yehuda v'Yisra-eil.
Go-aleinu, Adonai
Tz'va-ot sh'mo,
K'dosh Yisra-eil.

בָּרוּךְ אַתָּה, יי,
גָּאַל יִשְׂרָאֵל.

Baruch ata, Adonai,
ga-al Yisra-eil.

We praise You, Eternal God,
who freed our people Israel.

T'filah

תְּפִלָּה

PLEASE RISE

◆ GOD OF ALL GENERATIONS ◆ אָבוֹת וְאִמָּהוֹת

Baruch ata, Adonai,	בָּרוּךְ אַתָּה, יי,
Eloheinu veilohei	אֱלֹהֵינוּ וֵאלֹהֵי
avoteinu v'imoteinu.	אֲבוֹתֵינוּ וְאִמּוֹתֵינוּ.

Abraham and Sarah, Isaac and Rebekah,
Jacob and Rachel and Leah.
They are the fathers and mothers
of the Jewish people.

You were their God,
and You are our God, too.

We remember them, God,
and we know You do, too.

You protected them
and You took care of them.
Protect us, we pray,
and take care of us.

Baruch ata, Adonai,	בָּרוּךְ אַתָּה, יי,
magein Avraham	מָגֵן אַבְרָהָם
v'ezrat Sara.	וְעֶזְרַת שָׂרָה.

We praise You, Eternal God.
Like a shield,
You protect the Jewish people.

Ata gibor — אַתָּה גִּבּוֹר
l'olam, Adonai, — לְעוֹלָם, יי,
m'chayei hakol — מְחַיֵּה הַכֹּל
ata, rav l'hoshi-a. — אַתָּה, רַב לְהוֹשִׁיעַ.

You are mighty, God;
You give us life and hope.

M'chalkeil chayim — מְכַלְכֵּל חַיִּים
b'chesed, — בְּחֶסֶד,
m'chayei hakol — מְחַיֵּה הַכֹּל
b'rachamim rabim. — בְּרַחֲמִים רַבִּים.

With love and kindness,
You keep us alive.

Someich nof'lim, — סוֹמֵךְ נוֹפְלִים,
v'rofei cholim, — וְרוֹפֵא חוֹלִים,

You help us lift up those who fall;
You help us care for those who are sick.

umatir asurim, — וּמַתִּיר אֲסוּרִים,
um'kayeim emunato — וּמְקַיֵּם אֱמוּנָתוֹ
lisheinei afar. — לִישֵׁנֵי עָפָר.

You help us bring freedom.
You remember those who lived before us.

Mi chamocha
ba-al g'vurot,
umi domeh lach,
melech meimit
um'chayeh umatzmi-ach
y'shu-a?

מִי כָמְוֹךָ
בַּֽעַל גְּבוּרוֹת,
וּמִי דְּוֹמֶה לָּךְ,
מֶֽלֶךְ מֵמִית
וּמְחַיֶּה וּמַצְמִיחַ
יְשׁוּעָה?

Who is like You, mighty God?
Who can compare to You?

Baruch ata, Adonai,
m'chayei hakol.

בָּרוּךְ אַתָּה, יי,
מְחַיֵּה הַכֹּל.

Blessed are You, Eternal God.
You give life to all that lives!

God, everywhere we turn
we feel You with us.

Kadosh, kadosh, קָדוֹשׁ, קָדוֹשׁ,
kadosh. קָדוֹשׁ.

We feel You with us
when we see a newborn baby.

Holy, holy, holy.

We feel You with us
when we touch a soft flower.

Kadosh, kadosh, קָדוֹשׁ, קָדוֹשׁ,
kadosh. קָדוֹשׁ.

We feel You with us
when we see a rainbow after a storm.

Holy, holy, holy.

We feel You with us
when we are loving and loved.

Kadosh, kadosh, קָדוֹשׁ, קָדוֹשׁ,
kadosh. קָדוֹשׁ.

We feel You with us
when we do a mitzvah.

Holy, holy, holy.

קָדוֹשׁ, קָדוֹשׁ,
קָדוֹשׁ יהוה
צְבָאוֹת, מְלֹא
כָל־הָאָֽרֶץ
כְּבוֹדוֹ.

Kadosh, kadosh,
kadosh Adonai
Tz'va-ot, m'lo
chol ha-aretz
k'vodo.

בָּרוּךְ כְּבוֹד־
יהוה מִמְּקוֹמוֹ.

Baruch k'vod
Adonai mim'komo.

יִמְלֹךְ יהוה
לְעוֹלָם, אֱלֹהַֽיִךְ
צִיּוֹן, לְדֹר וָדֹר.
הַלְלוּיָהּ!

Yimloch Adonai
l'olam, Elohayich
Tziyon, l'dor vador.
Halleluyah!

בָּרוּךְ אַתָּה, יי,
הָאֵל הַקָּדוֹשׁ.

Baruch ata, Adonai,
ha-Eil hakadosh.

We praise You, Eternal God.
Everywhere we turn,
You are there.

PLEASE BE SEATED

◆ SHABBAT IS HOLY ◆ קְדוּשַּׁת הַיּוֹם

Today is a holy day.

Today is Shabbat

Today is a day to rest.

Today is a day to study Torah.

Today is a day to pray.

Today is a day to be with friends.

Thank You, God, for this holy day.

Thank You, God, for Shabbat.

Baruch ata, Adonai, m'kadeish ha-Shabbat.	בָּרוּךְ אַתָּה, יי, מְקַדֵּשׁ הַשַּׁבָּת.

We praise You, Eternal God.
You make Shabbat holy.

Yism'chu	יִשְׂמְחוּ
v'malchut'cha	בְמַלְכוּתְךָ
shom'rei Shabbat	שׁוֹמְרֵי שַׁבָּת
v'kor'ei oneg.	וְקוֹרְאֵי עֹנֶג.
Am m'kad'shei	עַם מְקַדְּשֵׁי
sh'vi-i, kulam	שְׁבִיעִי, כֻּלָּם
yisb'u v'yit-an'gu	יִשְׂבְּעוּ וְיִתְעַנְּגוּ
mituvecha.	מִטּוּבֶךָ.
V'hash'vi-i	וְהַשְּׁבִיעִי
ratzita bo	רָצִיתָ בּוֹ
v'kidashto.	וְקִדַּשְׁתּוֹ.
Chemdat yamim	חֶמְדַּת יָמִים
oto karata,	אוֹתוֹ קָרָאתָ,
zeicher l'ma-asei	זֵכֶר לְמַעֲשֵׂה
v'reishit.	בְרֵאשִׁית.

◆ **PRAYERS OF ASKING** ◆

O God,
You have made the world a special place.
Help us make good things happen
in the world.

You gave our people the Torah.
בָּרוּךְ אַתָּה, יי *Baruch ata, Adonai:*
Help us use Your book to learn wisdom.

You make healing possible.
בָּרוּךְ אַתָּה, יי *Baruch ata, Adonai:*
Help us heal those who are sick.

You show us how to learn
from our mistakes.

יי ,בָּרוּךְ אַתָּה *Baruch ata, Adonai:*
Help us say, "I'm sorry,"
and "I forgive you."

You make the soil rich to grow food.

יי ,בָּרוּךְ אַתָּה *Baruch ata, Adonai:*
Help us share with others.

You want people to be free.

יי ,בָּרוּךְ אַתָּה *Baruch ata, Adonai:*
Help us work for everyone's freedom.

You taught us about justice.

יי ,בָּרוּךְ אַתָּה *Baruch ata, Adonai:*
Help us always to be fair.

You love the Land of Israel and the
City of Jerusalem.

יי ,בָּרוּךְ אַתָּה *Baruch ata, Adonai:*
Help us work for our Jewish homeland.

You are near to all who call on You.

יי ,בָּרוּךְ אַתָּה *Baruch ata, Adonai:*
Help us know You are with us always.

◆◆

רְצֵה, יי אֱלֹהֵינוּ,
בְּעַמְּךָ יִשְׂרָאֵל,
וּתְפִלָּתָם בְּאַהֲבָה
תְקַבֵּל,
וּתְהִי לְרָצוֹן תָּמִיד
עֲבוֹדַת יִשְׂרָאֵל
עַמֶּךָ.

R'tsei, Adonai Eloheinu,
b'amcha Yisra-eil,
ut'filatam b'ahava
t'kabeil,
ut'hi l'ratson tamid
avodat yisra-eil
ameicha.

Hear our prayers, God,
and show us Your love.
Help us always to know
that You are everywhere.
Here and at home,
in the morning and at night,
whether happy or sad,
we can turn to You.
There is no God but You.

בָּרוּךְ אַתָּה, יי,
שֶׁאוֹתְךָ לְבַדְּךָ
בְּיִרְאָה נַעֲבוֹד.

Baruch ata, Adonai,
she-ot'cha l'vad'cha
b'yir-a na-avod.

We praise You, God.
We pray to You and You alone.

We thank You, God,
for all the blessings You give.

Life: it is filled with wonder.

The world: it is filled with beauty.

A soul: it is filled with mystery.

Every day—morning, noon, and night—
these remind us of You.

Baruch ata, Adonai,	בָּרוּךְ אַתָּה, יי,
hatov shimcha	הַטּוֹב שִׁמְךָ
ul'cha na-eh	וּלְךָ נָאֶה
l'hodot.	לְהוֹדוֹת.

We praise You, Eternal God,
for all these blessings You give us.

We pray for peace.

Peace for everyone, everywhere.

Peace for soldiers fighting wars.

Peace for people who live
where soldiers are fighting around them.

Peace for parents who are worried
about their children.

Peace for children who are worried
about their parents.

Peace for people who are struggling
with others.

Peace for people who are struggling
with themselves.

Baruch ata, Adonai, osei hashalom.	בָּרוּךְ אַתָּה, יי, עוֹשֵׂה הַשָּׁלוֹם.

We praise You, Eternal God.
You help us make peace.
And you help us find peace.

◆

Sim shalom, *tova uv'racha,* *chein vachesed* *v'rachamim.*	שִׂים שָׁלוֹם, טוֹבָה וּבְרָכָה, חֵן וָחֶסֶד וְרַחֲמִים.

◆◆

I have many feelings, God.

Some are good. Some are bad.

Sometimes I like my feelings.
Sometimes I don't.

Sometimes I understand my feelings.
Sometimes I don't.

Sometimes I can control my feelings.
Sometimes I can't.

I like having good feelings.
And I like to understand and control
my feelings.

Help me understand them.
And help me control them as I grow.

Yihyu l'ratzon	יִהְיוּ לְרָצוֹן
imrei fi,	אִמְרֵי־פִי
v'hegyon libi	וְהֶגְיוֹן לִבִּי
l'fanecha,	לְפָנֶיךָ,
Adonai, tzuri v'go-ali.	יהוה, צוּרִי וְגוֹאֲלִי.

May the words of my mouth
and the thoughts in my heart
be pleasing to You, O God.

(For a Torah reading, turn to page 89.)

(For Closing Prayers, turn to page 99.)

Seder K'ri-at Ha-Torah

The Torah is like
a precious jewel.
It sparkles with truth
and wisdom.
Let us take this jewel,
our Sefer Torah,
from the Ark
and hold it close.
Let us open it up
and read its words,
and learn from its wisdom
and truth.

PLEASE RISE

(Open the Ark)
(Take the Torah from the Ark)

Al sh'losha d'varim	עַל־שְׁלֹשָׁה דְבָרִים
ha-olam omeid:	הָעוֹלָם עוֹמֵד:
al ha-Torah,	עַל הַתּוֹרָה,
v'al ha-avoda,	וְעַל הָעֲבוֹדָה,
v'al g'milut	וְעַל גְּמִילוּת
chasadim.	חֲסָדִים.
Beit Ya'akov,	בֵּית יַעֲקֹב,
l'chu v'nel'cha	לְכוּ וְנֵלְכָה
b'or Adonai.	בְּאוֹר יהוה.

O House of Jacob, come:
let us walk together,
and God's light will shine before us.

(Hakafa might be here)

Sh'ma Yisra-eil:	שְׁמַע יִשְׂרָאֵל:
Adonai Eloheinu,	יהוה אֱלֹהֵינוּ,
Adonai echad!	יהוה אֶחָד!

Hear, O Israel: the Eternal One is our God, the Eternal God alone!

Echad Eloheinu,	אֶחָד אֱלֹהֵינוּ,
gadol Adoneinu,	גָּדוֹל אֲדוֹנֵינוּ,
kadosh sh'mo.	קָדוֹשׁ שְׁמוֹ.

Our God is One, Our God is great,
Holy is God's Name.

L'cha, Adonai,	לְךָ, יהוה,
hag'dula v'hag'vura	הַגְּדֻלָּה וְהַגְּבוּרָה
v'hatiferet	וְהַתִּפְאֶרֶת
v'haneitzach v'hahod,	וְהַנֵּצַח וְהַהוֹד,
ki chol bashamayim	כִּי כֹל בַּשָּׁמַיִם
uva-aretz.	וּבָאָרֶץ.
L'cha, Adonai,	לְךָ, יהוה,
hamamlacha	הַמַּמְלָכָה
v'hamitnasei	וְהַמִּתְנַשֵּׂא
l'chol l'rosh.	לְכֹל לְרֹאשׁ.

PLEASE BE SEATED

Reading of the Torah

BEFORE THE READING

Bar'chu et Adonai	בָּרְכוּ אֶת־יי
ham'vorach!	הַמְבֹרָךְ!
Baruch Adonai	בָּרוּךְ יי
ham'vorach	הַמְבֹרָךְ
l'olam va-ed!	לְעוֹלָם וָעֶד!
Baruch ata, Adonai	בָּרוּךְ אַתָּה, יי
Eloheinu, melech	אֱלֹהֵינוּ, מֶלֶךְ
ha-olam, asher	הָעוֹלָם, אֲשֶׁר
bachar banu	בָּחַר־בָּנוּ
mikol ha-amim,	מִכָּל־הָעַמִּים,
v'natan lanu	וְנָתַן־לָנוּ
et Torato.	אֶת־תּוֹרָתוֹ.
Baruch ata, Adonai,	בָּרוּךְ אַתָּה, יי,
notein ha-Torah.	נוֹתֵן הַתּוֹרָה.

Baruch ata,	בָּרוּךְ אַתָּה,
Adonai Eloheinu	יי אֱלֹהֵינוּ,
melech ha-olam,	מֶלֶךְ הָעוֹלָם,
asher natan lanu	אֲשֶׁר נָתַן לָנוּ
Torat emet,	תּוֹרַת אֱמֶת,
vechayei olam	וְחַיֵּי עוֹלָם
nata betocheinu.	נָטַע בְּתוֹכֵנוּ.
Baruch ata, Adonai,	בָּרוּךְ אַתָּה, יי,
notein ha-Torah.	נוֹתֵן הַתּוֹרָה.

Reading of the Haftarah

BEFORE THE READING

Baruch ata,	בָּרוּךְ אַתָּה,
Adonai Eloheinu,	יי אֱלֹהֵינוּ,
melech ha-olam,	מֶלֶךְ הָעוֹלָם,
asher bachar	אֲשֶׁר בָּחַר
bin'vi-im tovim,	בִּנְבִיאִים טוֹבִים,
v'ratza v'divreihem	וְרָצָה בְדִבְרֵיהֶם
hane-emarim	הַנֶּאֱמָרִים
be-emet.	בֶּאֱמֶת.
Baruch ata,	בָּרוּךְ אַתָּה,
Adonai, habocheir	יי, הַבּוֹחֵר
ba-Torah, uv'Mosheh	בַּתּוֹרָה, וּבְמֹשֶׁה
avdo, uv'Yisra-eil	עַבְדּוֹ, וּבְיִשְׂרָאֵל
amo, uvin'vi-ei	עַמּוֹ, וּבִנְבִיאֵי
ha-emet vatzedek.	הָאֱמֶת וָצֶדֶק.

AFTER THE READING

Baruch ata,	בָּרוּךְ אַתָּה,
Adonai Eloheinu,	יי אֱלֹהֵינוּ,
melech ha-olam,	מֶלֶךְ הָעוֹלָם,
tzur kol ha-olamim,	צוּר כָּל־הָעוֹלָמִים,
tzadik b'chol	צַדִּיק בְּכָל־
hadorot,	הַדּוֹרוֹת,
ha-Eil hane-eman,	הָאֵל הַנֶּאֱמָן,
ha-omeir v'oseh,	הָאוֹמֵר וְעוֹשֶׂה,

94
SEDER K'RI-AT
HA-TORAH
94
SEDER K'RI-AT
HA-TORAH
94
SEDER K'RI-AT
HA-TORAH

ham'dabeir um'kayeim,	הַמְדַבֵּר וּמְקַיֵּם,
shekol d'varav	שֶׁכָּל־דְּבָרָיו
emet vatzedek.	אֱמֶת וָצֶדֶק.
Al ha-Torah v'al	עַל־הַתּוֹרָה וְעַל־
ha-avoda v'al	הָעֲבוֹדָה וְעַל־
han'vi-im v'al yom	הַנְּבִיאִים וְעַל־יוֹם
ha-Shabbat hazeh,	הַשַּׁבָּת הַזֶּה,
shenatata lanu,	שֶׁנָּתַתָּ־לָּנוּ,
Adonai Eloheinu,	יי אֱלֹהֵינוּ,
lik'dusha v'lim'nucha,	לִקְדֻשָּׁה וְלִמְנוּחָה,
l'chavod ul'tif-aret,	לְכָבוֹד וּלְתִפְאָרֶת,
al hakol,	עַל־הַכֹּל,
Adonai Eloheinu,	יי אֱלֹהֵינוּ,
anachnu modim lach	אֲנַחְנוּ מוֹדִים לָךְ
um'var'chim otach.	וּמְבָרְכִים אוֹתָךְ.
Yitbarach shimcha	יִתְבָּרַךְ שִׁמְךָ
b'fi kol chai	בְּפִי כָּל־חַי
tamid l'olam va-ed.	תָּמִיד לְעוֹלָם וָעֶד.
Baruch ata, Adonai,	בָּרוּךְ אַתָּה, יי,
m'kadeish ha-Shabbat.	מְקַדֵּשׁ הַשַּׁבָּת.

Returning the Torah to the Ark

PLEASE RISE

This is our Torah.
Its words are the same ones
that our parents and grandparents read.
In all times and all places,
its words never change.
May our children and grandchildren,
and their children and grandchildren,
read its words as well.

Hodo al eretz	הוֹדוֹ עַל אֶרֶץ
v'shamayim,	וְשָׁמָיִם,
vayarem keren l'amo,	וַיָּרֶם קֶרֶן לְעַמּוֹ,
t'hila	תְּהִלָּה
l'chol chasidav,	לְכָל־חֲסִידָיו,
liv'nei Yisra-eil,	לִבְנֵי יִשְׂרָאֵל,
am k'rovo.	עַם קְרוֹבוֹ.
Halleluyah!	הַלְלוּיָהּ!

The Torah is a tree which gives us life.
Its words are like sweet fruit
that feed and delight us.
Its ways are pleasant,
and all its paths lead to peace.

Eitz chayim hi	עֵץ־חַיִּים הִיא
lamachazikim bah,	לַמַּחֲזִיקִים בָּהּ,
v'tom'cheha m'ushar.	וְתֹמְכֶיהָ מְאֻשָּׁר.
D'racheha	דְּרָכֶיהָ
darchei no-am,	דַּרְכֵי־נֹעַם,
v'chol n'tivoteha	וְכָל־נְתִיבוֹתֶיהָ
shalom.	שָׁלוֹם.
Hashiveinu, Adonai,	הֲשִׁיבֵנוּ, יהוה,
eilecha v'nashuva.	אֵלֶיךָ וְנָשׁוּבָה.
Chadeish yameinu	חַדֵּשׁ יָמֵינוּ
k'kedem.	כְּקֶדֶם.

Closing Prayers

◆ ALEINU I ◆ עָלֵֽינוּ – א׳

PLEASE RISE

Aleinu l'shabei-ach	עָלֵינוּ לְשַׁבֵּחַ
la-adon hakol,	לַאֲדוֹן הַכֹּל,
lateit g'dula	לָתֵת גְּדֻלָּה
l'yotzeir b'reishit,	לְיוֹצֵר בְּרֵאשִׁית,
shelo asanu	שֶׁלֹּא עָשָֽׂנוּ
k'goyei ha-aratzot	כְּגוֹיֵי הָאֲרָצוֹת,
v'lo samanu	וְלֹא שָׂמָֽנוּ
k'mishp'chot	כְּמִשְׁפְּחוֹת
ha-adama;	הָאֲדָמָה;
shelo sam	שֶׁלֹּא שָׂם
chelkeinu kahem	חֶלְקֵֽנוּ כָּהֶם,
v'goraleinu	וְגוֹרָלֵֽנוּ
k'chol hamonam.	כְּכָל־הֲמוֹנָם.
Va-anachnu kor'im	וַאֲנַֽחְנוּ כּוֹרְעִים
umishtachavim	וּמִשְׁתַּחֲוִים
umodim	וּמוֹדִים
lifnei melech	לִפְנֵי מֶֽלֶךְ
malchei ham'lachim,	מַלְכֵי הַמְּלָכִים,
ha-Kadosh	הַקָּדוֹשׁ
Baruch Hu.	בָּרוּךְ הוּא.

We pray that some day
the world will be at peace.
Then everyone will be free
to pray to only You, God.
May that great time come soon.

V'ne-emar:	וְנֶאֱמַר:
v'haya Adonai	וְהָיָה יהוה
l'melech	לְמֶלֶךְ
al kol ha-aretz.	עַל־כָּל־הָאָרֶץ;
Bayom hahu	בַּיּוֹם הַהוּא
yihyeh Adonai echad	יִהְיֶה יהוה אֶחָד
ush'mo echad.	וּשְׁמוֹ אֶחָד.

(Kaddish begins on page 102.)

Let us adore the ever-living God,
and render praise unto God,
Who spread out the heavens
and established the earth,
Whose glory is revealed
in the heavens above,
and Whose greatness is manifest
throughout the world.
You are our God, there is none else.

Va-anachnu kor'im וַאֲנַחְנוּ כּוֹרְעִים
umishtachavim וּמִשְׁתַּחֲוִים
umodim lifnei melech וּמוֹדִים לִפְנֵי מֶלֶךְ
malchei ham'lachim, מַלְכֵי הַמְּלָכִים,
ha-Kadosh הַקָּדוֹשׁ
Baruch Hu. בָּרוּךְ הוּא.

We pray that some day
the world will be at peace.
Then everyone will be free
to pray to only You, God.
May that great time come soon.

V'ne-emar: וְנֶאֱמַר:
v'haya Adonai l'melech וְהָיָה יהוה לְמֶלֶךְ
al kol ha-aretz. עַל־כָּל־הָאָרֶץ.
Bayom hahu בַּיּוֹם הַהוּא
yihyeh Adonai echad יִהְיֶה יהוה אֶחָד
ush'mo echad. וּשְׁמוֹ אֶחָד.

At this time,
we think about people who have died.

Some were our family.

Some were our friends.

When we think about these people,
we miss them.

We are grateful for memories of them.

We thank You, God,
for life and for the people we have loved.

יִתְגַּדַּל וְיִתְקַדַּשׁ שְׁמֵהּ רַבָּא

Yitgadal v'yitkadash sh'mei raba

בְּעָלְמָא דִּי־בְרָא כִרְעוּתֵהּ,

b'alma di v'ra chir'utei,

וְיַמְלִיךְ מַלְכוּתֵהּ

v'yamlich malchutei

בְּחַיֵּיכוֹן וּבְיוֹמֵיכוֹן

b'chayeichon uv'yomeichon

וּבְחַיֵּי דְכָל־בֵּית יִשְׂרָאֵל,

uv'chayei dechol beit Yisra-eil,

בַּעֲגָלָא וּבִזְמַן קָרִיב, וְאִמְרוּ: אָמֵן.

ba-agala uviz'man kariv, v'imru: Amein.

יְהֵא שְׁמֵהּ רַבָּא מְבָרַךְ

Y'hei sh'mei raba m'varach

לְעָלַם וּלְעָלְמֵי עָלְמַיָּא.

l'alam ul'almei almaya.

יִתְבָּרַךְ וְיִשְׁתַּבַּח,

Yitbarach v'yishtabach,

וְיִתְפָּאַר וְיִתְרוֹמַם וְיִתְנַשֵּׂא,

v'yitpa-ar v'yitromam v'yitnasei,

וְיִתְהַדַּר וְיִתְעַלֶּה וְיִתְהַלַּל

v'yithadar v'yit-aleh v'yithalal

שְׁמֵהּ דְּקוּדְשָׁא, בְּרִיךְ הוּא,

sh'mei d'kud'sha, b'rich hu,

לְעֵֽלָּא מִן־כָּל־בִּרְכָתָא וְשִׁירָתָא,

l'eila min kol birchata v'shirata,

תֻּשְׁבְּחָתָא וְנֶחֱמָתָא

tushb'chata v'nechemata

דַּאֲמִירָן בְּעָלְמָא, וְאִמְרוּ: אָמֵן.

da-amiran b'alma, ve-im'ru: Amein.

יְהֵא שְׁלָמָא רַבָּא

Y'hei sh'lama raba

מִן־שְׁמַיָּא וְחַיִּים עָלֵֽינוּ

min sh'maya v'chayim aleinu

וְעַל־כָּל־יִשְׂרָאֵל, וְאִמְרוּ: אָמֵן.

v'al kol Yisra-eil, v'im'ru: Amein.

עֹשֶׂה שָׁלוֹם בִּמְרוֹמָיו,

Oseh shalom bim'romav,

הוּא יַעֲשֶׂה שָׁלוֹם עָלֵֽינוּ

hu ya-aseh shalom aleinu

וְעַל כָּל־יִשְׂרָאֵל, וְאִמְרוּ: אָמֵן.

v'al kol Yisra-eil, ve-im'ru: Amein.

105 KIDDUSH
105 KIDDUSH
105 KIDDUSH
105 KIDDUSH

Kiddush

FOR EREV SHABBAT

Like wine, Shabbat is sweet.
We lift this cup to celebrate
the love of family and
the joy of living.
We sing the Kiddush
and taste the wine
to remind us that Shabbat
is a day of sweetness and love.

We praise You,
Eternal our God,
Creator of the
fruit of the vine.

בָּרוּךְ אַתָּה,
יי אֱלֹהֵינוּ,
מֶלֶךְ הָעוֹלָם,
בּוֹרֵא פְּרִי הַגָּפֶן.

Baruch ata,
Adonai Eloheinu,
melech ha-olam,
borei p'ri hagafen.

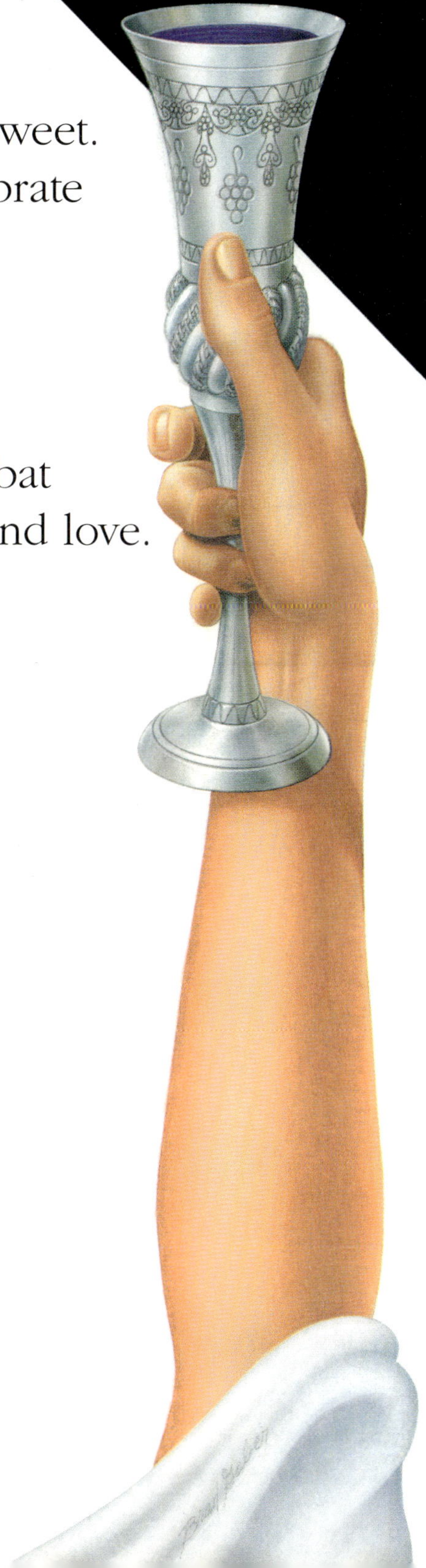

106 KIDDUSH
106 KIDDUSH
106 KIDDUSH
106 KIDDUSH

Baruch ata,	בָּרוּךְ אַתָּה,
Adonai Eloheinu,	יי אֱלֹהֵינוּ,
melech ha-olam,	מֶלֶךְ הָעוֹלָם,
asher kid'shanu	אֲשֶׁר קִדְּשָׁנוּ
b'mitzvotav	בְּמִצְוֹתָיו
v'ratza vanu,	וְרָצָה בָנוּ,
v'Shabbat kodsho	וְשַׁבַּת קָדְשׁוֹ
b'ahava uv'ratzon	בְּאַהֲבָה וּבְרָצוֹן
hinchilanu,	הִנְחִילָנוּ,
zikaron l'ma-asei	זִכָּרוֹן לְמַעֲשֵׂה
v'reishit.	בְרֵאשִׁית.
Ki hu yom	כִּי הוּא יוֹם
t'chila	תְּחִלָּה
l'mikra-ei kodesh,	לְמִקְרָאֵי קֹדֶשׁ,
zecher litzi-at	זֵכֶר לִיצִיאַת
Mitzrayim.	מִצְרָיִם.
Ki vanu vacharta	כִּי־בָנוּ בָחַרְתָּ
v'otanu kidashta	וְאוֹתָנוּ קִדַּשְׁתָּ
mikol ha-amim,	מִכָּל־הָעַמִּים,
v'Shabbat kodsh'cha,	וְשַׁבַּת קָדְשְׁךָ
b'ahava uv'ratzon	בְּאַהֲבָה וּבְרָצוֹן
hinchaltanu.	הִנְחַלְתָּנוּ.
Baruch ata, Adonai,	בָּרוּךְ אַתָּה, יי,
m'kadeish ha-Shabbat.	מְקַדֵּשׁ הַשַּׁבָּת.

God gave us Shabbat
to rest from our work,
and to remember
that God freed us from Egypt.
This is a day of joy and love.

V'sham'ru	וְשָׁמְרוּ
v'nei Yisra-eil	בְנֵי־יִשְׂרָאֵל
et ha-Shabbat,	אֶת־הַשַּׁבָּת,
la-asot et ha-Shabbat	לַעֲשׂוֹת אֶת־הַשַּׁבָּת
l'dorotam	לְדֹרֹתָם
b'rit olam.	בְּרִית עוֹלָם.
Beini uvein	בֵּינִי וּבֵין
b'nei Yisra-eil	בְּנֵי יִשְׂרָאֵל
ot hi l'olam.	אוֹת הִיא לְעֹלָם.
Ki sheishet yamim	כִּי שֵׁשֶׁת יָמִים
asa Adonai	עָשָׂה יהוה
et hashamayim	אֶת־הַשָּׁמַיִם
v'et ha-aretz,	וְאֶת־הָאָרֶץ,
uvayom hash'vi-i	וּבַיּוֹם הַשְּׁבִיעִי
shavat vayinafash.	שָׁבַת וַיִּנָּפַשׁ.

Al kein beirach	עַל־כֵּן בֵּרַךְ
Adonai et yom	יהוה אֶת־יוֹם
ha-Shabbat	הַשַּׁבָּת
vay'kad'sheihu.	וַיְקַדְּשֵׁהוּ.

Baruch ata,	בָּרוּךְ אַתָּה,
Adonai Eloheinu,m	יי אֱלֹהֵינוּ,
melech ha-olam,	מֶלֶךְ הָעוֹלָם,
borei p'ri hagafen.	בּוֹרֵא פְּרִי הַגָּפֶן.

Motzi

Baruch ata,	בָּרוּךְ אַתָּה,
Adonai Eloheinu,	יי אֱלֹהֵינוּ,
melech ha-olam,	מֶלֶךְ הָעוֹלָם,
hamotzi lechem	הַמּוֹצִיא לֶחֶם
min ha-aretz.	מִן הָאָרֶץ.

For Older Children

"Words of Our Mouths, Thoughts of Our Hearts"

A Service for Shabbat and Weekdays

OPENING MUSIC

◆◆

We have come together to share and to sing. Our words are prayers. Our prayers are about the most important things in our lives and the people we love. When we pray, we talk to God. Sometimes we say our prayers so that our friends can also hear them, and sometimes we listen carefully to ourselves.

This place, too, is special. When Jews gather together to pray, that place becomes holy. This place is holy.

Before we begin, we must be very quiet . . . and listen.
The air around us is filled with sound:
our breathing, in and out;
the beating of our hearts;
many secret, little sounds.

But we only hear when we open our ears
. . . and our minds . . . and our hearts.
Maybe we even hear that God is with us
as we prepare to pray.

Be very still now.
Concentrate.
Listen.

◆◆

Candle Blessing

FOR SHABBAT

We praise You, God, Ruler of the world.
You make us holy with mitzvot,
and so we light the candles of Shabbat.

Baruch ata,	בָּרוּךְ אַתָּה,
Adonai Eloheinu,	יי אֱלֹהֵינוּ,
melech ha-olam,	מֶלֶךְ הָעוֹלָם,
asher kid'shanu	אֲשֶׁר קִדְּשָׁנוּ
b'mitzvotav	בְּמִצְוֹתָיו
v'tzivanu l'hadlik	וְצִוָּנוּ לְהַדְלִיק
neir shel Shabbat.	נֵר שֶׁל שַׁבָּת.

Sh'ma and Its Blessings

שְׁמַע וּבִרְכוֹתֶיהָ

We rise and pray.

בָּרְכוּ אֶת־יי הַמְבֹרָךְ!

Praise God to whom our praise is due.

Baruch Adonai ham'vorach	בָּרוּךְ יי הַמְבֹרָךְ
l'olam va-ed!	לְעוֹלָם וָעֶד!

Praised be God to whom our praise is due,
now and forever.

FOR AN EVENING SERVICE — מַעֲרִיב עֲרָבִים

Baruch ata, Adonai	בָּרוּךְ אַתָּה, יי
Eloheinu, melech ha-olam,	אֱלֹהֵינוּ, מֶלֶךְ הָעוֹלָם,
asher bid'varo	אֲשֶׁר בִּדְבָרוֹ
ma-ariv aravim,	מַעֲרִיב עֲרָבִים,
b'chochma pote-ach	בְּחָכְמָה פּוֹתֵחַ
sh'arim,	שְׁעָרִים,
uvit'vuna m'shaneh itim,	וּבִתְבוּנָה מְשַׁנֶּה עִתִּים,
umachalif et haz'manim,	וּמַחֲלִיף אֶת־הַזְּמַנִּים,
um'sadeir et hakochavim	וּמְסַדֵּר אֶת־הַכּוֹכָבִים
b'mishm'roteihem	בְּמִשְׁמְרוֹתֵיהֶם
baraki-a kir'tzono.	בָּרָקִיעַ כִּרְצוֹנוֹ.
Borei yom valaila,	בּוֹרֵא יוֹם וָלָיְלָה,
goleil or mip'nei choshech	גּוֹלֵל אוֹר מִפְּנֵי חֹשֶׁךְ
v'choshech mip'nei or,	וְחֹשֶׁךְ מִפְּנֵי אוֹר,
uma-avir yom	וּמַעֲבִיר יוֹם
umeivi laila, umavdil	וּמֵבִיא לָיְלָה, וּמַבְדִּיל
bein yom uvein laila,	בֵּין יוֹם וּבֵין לָיְלָה,
Adonai T'zvaot sh'mo.	יי צְבָאוֹת שְׁמוֹ.
Eil chai v'kayam,	אֵל חַי וְקַיָּם,
tamid yimloch aleinu,	תָּמִיד יִמְלֹךְ עָלֵינוּ
l'olam va-ed.	לְעוֹלָם וָעֶד.
Baruch ata, Adonai,	בָּרוּךְ אַתָּה, יי,
hama-ariv aravim.	הַמַּעֲרִיב עֲרָבִים.

We look at the world that God created.
Our world is filled with wonders.

Each day, we are blessed with air to breathe,
water to drink and food to eat.
We have places to live and people who love us.
This is a wonderful world. "Thank You, God!"

FOR A MORNING SERVICE — יוֹצֵר

Baruch ata,	בָּרוּךְ אַתָּה,
Adonai Eloheinu,	יי אֱלֹהֵינוּ,
melech ha-olam,	מֶלֶךְ הָעוֹלָם,
yotzeir or uvorei choshech,	יוֹצֵר אוֹר וּבוֹרֵא חֹשֶׁךְ,
oseh shalom	עֹשֶׂה שָׁלוֹם
uvorei et hakol.	וּבוֹרֵא אֶת־הַכֹּל.
Hamei-ir la-aretz v'ladarim	הַמֵּאִיר לָאָרֶץ וְלַדָּרִים
aleha b'rachamim,	עָלֶיהָ בְּרַחֲמִים,
uv'tuvo m'chadeish	וּבְטוּבוֹ מְחַדֵּשׁ
b'chol yom tamid	בְּכָל־יוֹם תָּמִיד
ma-asei v'reishit.	מַעֲשֵׂה בְרֵאשִׁית.
Ma rabu ma-asecha, Adonai!	מָה רַבּוּ מַעֲשֶׂיךָ, יי!
Kulam b'chochma asita,	כֻּלָּם בְּחָכְמָה עָשִׂיתָ,
mal'a ha-aretz kinyanecha.	מָלְאָה הָאָרֶץ קִנְיָנֶךָ.
Titbarach,	תִּתְבָּרַךְ,
Adonai Eloheinu,	יי אֱלֹהֵינוּ,
al shevach	עַל־שֶׁבַח
ma-asei yadecha	מַעֲשֵׂה יָדֶיךָ
v'al m'orei or she-asita:	וְעַל־מְאוֹרֵי־אוֹר שֶׁעָשִׂיתָ:
y'fa-arucha. Sela.	יְפָאֲרוּךָ. סֶּלָה.
Baruch ata, Adonai,	בָּרוּךְ אַתָּה, יי,
Yotzeir ham'orot.	יוֹצֵר הַמְּאוֹרוֹת.

We praise You, God, Ruler of the world,
who creates light and darkness,
who plans and forms all things.
We are grateful, God,
for this beautiful world in which we live.

We wonder: What is the right way to live?
Are there certain mitzvot we should do?
Can our daily lives be as special
as the world we have been given?

We learn what to do from You, God.
You teach us in Torah what is right and what is good.
You show Your love for us by giving us mitzvot.
We thank You for helping us lead good lives.

FOR AN EVENING SERVICE — אַהֲבַת עוֹלָם

Ahavat olam	אַהֲבַת עוֹלָם
beit Yisra-eil	בֵּית יִשְׂרָאֵל
am'cha ahavta.	עַמְּךָ אָהָבְתָּ.
Torah umitzvot,	תּוֹרָה וּמִצְוֹת,
chukim umishpatim	חֻקִּים וּמִשְׁפָּטִים
otanu limad'ta.	אוֹתָנוּ לִמַּדְתָּ.
Al kein,	עַל כֵּן,
Adonai Eloheinu,	יי אֱלֹהֵינוּ,
b'shochbeinu uv'kumeinu	בְּשָׁכְבֵנוּ וּבְקוּמֵנוּ
nasi-ach b'chukecha,	נָשִׂיחַ בְּחֻקֶּיךָ,
v'nismach b'divrei	וְנִשְׂמַח בְּדִבְרֵי
Torat'cha uv'mitzvotecha	תוֹרָתְךָ וּבְמִצְוֹתֶיךָ
l'olam va-ed.	לְעוֹלָם וָעֶד.
Ki heim chayeinu	כִּי הֵם חַיֵּינוּ
v'orech yameinu,	וְאֹרֶךְ יָמֵינוּ,
uvahem nehgeh	וּבָהֶם נֶהְגֶּה
yomam valaila.	יוֹמָם וָלָיְלָה.
V'ahavat'cha al tasir	וְאַהֲבָתְךָ אַל תָּסִיר
mimenu l'olamim!	מִמֶּנּוּ לְעוֹלָמִים!
Baruch ata, Adonai,	בָּרוּךְ אַתָּה, יי,
oheiv amo Yisra-eil.	אוֹהֵב עַמּוֹ יִשְׂרָאֵל.

Ahava raba ahavtanu,	אַהֲבָה רַבָּה אֲהַבְתָּנוּ,
Adonai Eloheinu,	יי אֱלֹהֵינוּ,
chemla g'dola viteira	חֶמְלָה גְדוֹלָה וִיתֵרָה
chamalta aleinu.	חָמַלְתָּ עָלֵינוּ.
Avinu malkeinu,	אָבִינוּ מַלְכֵּנוּ,
ba-avur avoteinu	בַּעֲבוּר אֲבוֹתֵינוּ
shebat'chu v'cha	שֶׁבָּטְחוּ בְךָ
vat'lam'dem	וַתְּלַמְּדֵם
chukei chayim,	חֻקֵּי חַיִּים,
kein t'choneinu	כֵּן תְּחָנֵּנוּ
ut'lam'deinu.	וּתְלַמְּדֵנוּ.
Baruch ata, Adonai,	בָּרוּךְ אַתָּה, יי,
habocheir b'amo	הַבּוֹחֵר בְּעַמּוֹ
Yisra-eil b'ahava.	יִשְׂרָאֵל בְּאַהֲבָה.

Your love and Your Torah help us know
that we are Jews. We praise You, God,
who in love has chosen Your people, Israel,
to serve you.

We promise to love You
and to use Your gift of Torah.
So, we pray:

שמע ישראל יהוה אלהינו יהוה אחד

Hear, O Israel: the Eternal One is our God,
the Eternal God alone!

Baruch sheim	בָּרוּךְ שֵׁם
k'vod malchuto	כְּבוֹד מַלְכוּתוֹ
l'olam va-ed!	לְעוֹלָם וָעֶד!

Blessed is God's glorious majesty for ever and ever!

PLEASE BE SEATED

V'ahavta et	וְאָהַבְתָּ אֵת
Adonai Elohecha	יהוה אֱלֹהֶיךָ
b'chol l'vav'cha,	בְּכָל־לְבָבְךָ,
uv'chol nafsh'cha,	וּבְכָל־נַפְשְׁךָ,
uv'chol m'odecha.	וּבְכָל־מְאֹדֶךָ.
V'hayu had'varim ha-eileh	וְהָיוּ הַדְּבָרִים הָאֵלֶּה
asher anochi m'tzav'cha	אֲשֶׁר אָנֹכִי מְצַוְּךָ
hayom al l'vavecha.	הַיּוֹם עַל־לְבָבֶךָ.
V'shinantam l'vanecha	וְשִׁנַּנְתָּם לְבָנֶיךָ
v'dibarta bam	וְדִבַּרְתָּ בָּם
b'shivt'cha b'veitecha,	בְּשִׁבְתְּךָ בְּבֵיתֶךָ,
uv'lecht'cha vaderech,	וּבְלֶכְתְּךָ בַדֶּרֶךְ,
uv'shochb'cha uv'kumecha.	וּבְשָׁכְבְּךָ וּבְקוּמֶךָ.

Uk'shartam l'ot	וּקְשַׁרְתָּם לְאוֹת
al yadecha,	עַל־יָדֶךָ,
v'hayu l'totafot	וְהָיוּ לְטֹטָפוֹת
bein einecha.	בֵּין עֵינֶיךָ.

וּכְתַבְתָּם עַל־מְזוּזֹת — *Uch'tavtam al m'zu-zot*
בֵּיתֶךָ וּבִשְׁעָרֶיךָ. — *beitecha uvish'arecha.*

לְמַעַן תִּזְכְּרוּ וַעֲשִׂיתֶם — *L'ma-an tizk'ru va-asitem*
אֶת־כָּל־מִצְוֹתָי, — *et kol mitzvotai,*
וִהְיִיתֶם קְדשִׁים — *vih'yitem k'doshim*
לֵאלֹהֵיכֶם. — *leiloheichem.*
אֲנִי יהוה אֱלֹהֵיכֶם, — *Ani Adonai Eloheichem,*
אֲשֶׁר הוֹצֵאתִי אֶתְכֶם — *asher hotzeiti etchem*
מֵאֶרֶץ מִצְרַיִם — *me-Eretz Mitzrayim*
לִהְיוֹת לָכֶם לֵאלֹהִים. — *lihyot lachem leilohim.*
אֲנִי יהוה אֱלֹהֵיכֶם. — *Ani Adonai Eloheichem.*

You shall love God with all your mind,
with all your strength, with all your being.

Set these words which I command you this day
upon your heart.
Teach them faithfully to your children;
speak about them in your home
and when you are away,
when you lie down and when you get up.

Bind them as a sign upon your hand;
let them be a symbol before your eyes;
write them on the doorposts of your house
and on your gates.

Remember My mitzvot, and do them.
In this way, you become holy.
I freed your people from Egyptian slavery long ago,
so that you might be My People.

I am the Eternal One, your God.

When our people were slaves in Egypt, they prayed to God for help. God freed them. Our people sang out with respect and love.

Today, as well, we trust God to help us. We dream of a better tomorrow. We sing those words our ancestors sang when they crossed the Sea of Reeds.

Mi chamocha	מִי־כָמֹכָה
ba-eilim, Adonai?	בָּאֵלִם, יהוה?
Mi kamocha	מִי כָּמֹכָה,
ne-dar bakodesh,	נֶאְדָּר בַּקֹּדֶשׁ,
nora t'hilot,	נוֹרָא תְהִלֹּת,
osei feleh?	עֹשֵׂה פֶלֶא?

Who is like you, Adonai?
No one is as holy and as wonderful as You.

When the Jewish people were freed from Pharaoh's oppression and slavery, they declared Adonai would be our God forever.

Adonai yimloch	יהוה יִמְלֹךְ
l'olam va-ed!	לְעֹלָם וָעֶד!

Baruch ata, Adonai,	בָּרוּךְ אַתָּה, יי,
ga-al Yisra-eil.	גָּאַל יִשְׂרָאֵל.

O God, as You helped our people before,
we pray that You will shelter and protect us now.
We praise You, God, who saves our people, Israel.

T'filah

תְּפִלָּה

PLEASE RISE

Adonai, s'fatai tiftach,	יי, שְׂפָתַי תִּפְתָּח,
ufi yagid t'hilatecha.	וּפִי יַגִּיד תְּהִלָּתֶךָ.

Eternal God, open my lips,
that my mouth may declare your glory.

◆ GOD OF ALL GENERATIONS ◆ אָבוֹת וְאִמָּהוֹת

Baruch ata, Adonai,	בָּרוּךְ אַתָּה, יי,
Eloheinu veilohei	אֱלֹהֵינוּ וֵאלֹהֵי
avoteinu v'imoteinu:	אֲבוֹתֵינוּ וְאִמּוֹתֵינוּ:
Elohei Avraham,	אֱלֹהֵי אַבְרָהָם,
Elohei Yitzchak,	אֱלֹהֵי יִצְחָק,
veilohei Ya-akov.	וֵאלֹהֵי יַעֲקֹב.
Elohei Sara,	אֱלֹהֵי שָׂרָה,
Elohei Rivka,	אֱלֹהֵי רִבְקָה,
Elohei Lei-a,	אֱלֹהֵי לֵאָה,
veilohei Racheil.	וֵאלֹהֵי רָחֵל.

הָאֵל הַגָּדוֹל הַגִּבּוֹר	*Ha-eil hagadol hagibor*
וְהַנּוֹרָא, אֵל עֶלְיוֹן,	*v'hanora, eil elyon,*
גּוֹמֵל חֲסָדִים טוֹבִים	*gomeil chasadim tovim*
וְקוֹנֵה הַכֹּל,	*v'konei hakol,*
וְזוֹכֵר חַסְדֵי	*v'zocheir chasdei*
אָבוֹת וְאִמָּהוֹת,	*avot v'imahot,*
וּמֵבִיא גְאֻלָּה	*umeivi g'ula*
לִבְנֵי בְנֵיהֶם,	*liv'nei v'neihem,*
לְמַעַן שְׁמוֹ בְּאַהֲבָה.	*l'ma-an sh'mo b'ahava.*
מֶלֶךְ עוֹזֵר	*Melech ozeir*
וּמוֹשִׁיעַ וּמָגֵן.	*umoshi-a umagein.*
בָּרוּךְ אַתָּה, יי,	*Baruch ata, Adonai,*
מָגֵן אַבְרָהָם	*magein Avraham*
וְעֶזְרַת שָׂרָה.	*v'ezrat Sara.*

We praise You, our God. Abraham, Isaac and Jacob, Sarah, Rebekah, Leah and Rachel—each of them prayed to You and praised You. You have always loved and protected us. We thank You for all that You have done, and we praise You, our Shield and our Protector.

Ata gibor l'olam,	אַתָּה גִּבּוֹר לְעוֹלָם,
Adonai, m'chayei hakol	יי, מְחַיֵּה הַכֹּל
ata, rav l'hoshi-a.	אַתָּה, רַב לְהוֹשִׁיעַ.
M'chalkeil chayim b'chesed,	מְכַלְכֵּל חַיִּים בְּחֶסֶד,
m'chayei hakol	מְחַיֵּה הַכֹּל
b'rachamim rabim.	בְּרַחֲמִים רַבִּים.
Someich nof'lim,	סוֹמֵךְ נוֹפְלִים,
v'rofei cholim,	וְרוֹפֵא חוֹלִים,
umatir asurim,	וּמַתִּיר אֲסוּרִים,
um'kayeim emunato	וּמְקַיֵּם אֱמוּנָתוֹ
lisheinei afar.	לִישֵׁנֵי עָפָר.
Mi chamocha ba-al g'vurot,	מִי כָמְוֹךָ בַּעַל גְּבוּרוֹת,
umi domeh lach,	וּמִי דְּוֹמֶה לָּךְ,
melech meimit um'chayeh	מֶלֶךְ מֵמִית וּמְחַיֶּה
umatzmiach y'shu-a?	וּמַצְמִיחַ יְשׁוּעָה?
V'ne-eman ata	וְנֶאֱמָן אַתָּה
l'hachayot hakol.	לְהַחֲיוֹת הַכֹּל.
Baruch ata, Adonai,	בָּרוּךְ אַתָּה, יי,
m'chayei hakol.	מְחַיֵּה הַכֹּל.

O God, as we remember all You do, we make this promise: to be like You. We will raise up those who fall, heal those who are sick, free those who are in need. As Your partners, we will support the poor, feed the hungry, house the homeless, befriend the lonely and give hope to all people. We will be faithful Jews.

As you have helped us live better lives, we shall help others. We praise You, O God, who gives meaning to our lives.

FOR AN EVENING SERVICE

אַתָּה קָדוֹשׁ
וְשִׁמְךָ קָדוֹשׁ,
וּקְדוֹשִׁים בְּכָל־יוֹם
יְהַלְלוּךָ, סֶּלָה.
בָּרוּךְ אַתָּה, יי,
הָאֵל הַקָּדוֹשׁ.

Ata kadosh
v'shimcha kadosh,
uk'doshim b'chol yom
y'hal'lucha, sela.
Baruch ata, Adonai,
ha-Eil hakadosh.

O God, You are holy. We speak of You every day.
We praise You, the holy God.

FOR A MORNING SERVICE

We raise our voices to sing of Your holiness.

קָדוֹשׁ, קָדוֹשׁ, קָדוֹשׁ
יהוה צְבָאוֹת,
מְלֹא כָל־הָאָרֶץ
כְּבוֹדוֹ.

Kadosh, kadosh, kadosh
Adonai tz'va-ot,
m'lo chol ha-aretz
k'vodo.

Holy, holy, holy is God;
the whole world is alive with Your glory.

בָּרוּךְ כְּבוֹד־יהוה
מִמְּקוֹמוֹ.

Baruch k'vod Adonai
mim'komo.

May You always be our God, now and for all time.

יִמְלֹךְ יהוה לְעוֹלָם,
אֱלֹהַיִךְ צִיּוֹן,
לְדֹר וָדֹר. הַלְלוּיָהּ!

Yimloch Adonai l'olam,
Elohayich Tziyon,
l'dor vador. Halleluyah!

PLEASE BE SEATED

(On Shabbat, continue on page 130.)

◆◆

(These blessings might be read in unison.)

◆ FOR UNDERSTANDING ◆ בִּינָה

You give us wisdom and teach us understanding.
We praise You, God, Giver of knowledge.

Baruch ata, Adonai,	בָּרוּךְ אַתָּה, יי,
chonein hada-at.	חוֹנֵן הַדָּעַת.

◆ FOR REPENTANCE ◆ תְּשׁוּבָה

Help us, God, to be sorry for wrongs we have done
and to improve our lives by turning to Your Torah.
We praise You, God. In Your love, You help us to grow.

Baruch ata, Adonai,	בָּרוּךְ אַתָּה, יי,
harotzeh bit'shuva.	הָרוֹצֶה בִּתְשׁוּבָה.

◆ FOR FORGIVENESS ◆ סְלִיחָה

Forgive us, God, when we make mistakes,
for we try to do right.
We praise You, God. You are quick to forgive.

Baruch ata, Adonai,	בָּרוּךְ אַתָּה, יי,
chanun hamarbeh	חַנּוּן הַמַּרְבֶּה
lislo-ach.	לִסְלוֹחַ.

◆ **FOR REDEMPTION** ◆ גְאוּלָה

O God, notice that Israel needs You,
and redeem us speedily.
We praise You, God, Redeemer of Israel.

Baruch ata, Adonai,	בָּרוּךְ אַתָּה, יי,
go-eil Yisra-eil.	גּוֹאֵל יִשְׂרָאֵל.

◆ **FOR HEALING** ◆ רְפוּאָה

When we are sick, God, help us get better.
We praise You, God, who heals the sick.

Baruch ata, Adonai,	בָּרוּךְ אַתָּה, יי,
rofei hacholim.	רוֹפֵא הַחוֹלִים.

◆ **FOR ABUNDANCE** ◆ בִּרְכַּת הַשָּׁנִים

Bless this year, God, by helping the earth
to bring forth food for everyone.
We pray that all children will have enough to eat.
We praise You, God, for You create a world
with enough for all to share.

Baruch ata, Adonai,	בָּרוּךְ אַתָּה, יי,
m'vareich hashanim.	מְבָרֵךְ הַשָּׁנִים.

◆ **FOR FREEDOM** ◆ חֵרוּת

Sound the great shofar to let us know
that freedom is here for all.
Let the song of liberty be heard everywhere!
We praise You, God, who brings freedom
to the oppressed.

Baruch ata, Adonai,	בָּרוּךְ אַתָּה, יי,
podeh ashukim.	פּוֹדֶה עֲשׁוּקִים.

◆ FOR THE GOVERNMENT ◆ מִשְׁפָּט

O God, as You rule with justice, so may You guide
the leaders of our nation and all lands.
May they govern with fairness.
We praise You, God, who loves justice.

Baruch ata, Adonai,	בָּרוּךְ אַתָּה, יְיָ,
melech oheiv tz'daka	מֶלֶךְ אוֹהֵב צְדָקָה
umishpat.	וּמִשְׁפָּט.

◆ ON EVIL ◆ עַל הָרִשְׁעָה

Let evil be no more.
Help us bring goodness to our world.
We praise You, God,
who wants evil to disappear from the earth.

Baruch ata, Adonai,	בָּרוּךְ אַתָּה, יְיָ,
hamashbit resha	הַמַּשְׁבִּית רֶשַׁע
min ha-aretz.	מִן־הָאָרֶץ.

◆ THE RIGHTEOUS ◆ עַל הַצַּדִּיקִים

We pray that You will count us among those
who have done good with their lives.
We praise You, God, who supports people
who work to do right.

Baruch ata, Adonai,	בָּרוּךְ אַתָּה, יְיָ,
mish-an umivtach	מִשְׁעָן וּמִבְטָח
latzadikim.	לַצַּדִּיקִים.

◆ **FOR JERUSALEM** ◆ בּוֹנֵה יְרוּשָׁלָיִם

Bring peace to the land of Israel and all who live there.
May it be a land of Torah.
We praise You, God, who gives peace to Jerusalem.

Baruch ata, Adonai,	בָּרוּךְ אַתָּה, יְיָ,
boneh Y'rushalayim.	בּוֹנֵה יְרוּשָׁלָיִם

◆ **DELIVERANCE** ◆ יְשׁוּעָה

As light reveals a path in the darkness,
so may Your light help us find the way to You.
We praise You, God, who will cause
the light of deliverance to shine for all the world.

Baruch ata, Adonai,	בָּרוּךְ אַתָּה, יְיָ,
matzmi-ach keren y'shu-a.	מַצְמִיחַ קֶרֶן יְשׁוּעָה.

◆ **FOR OUR PRAYERS** ◆ שׁוֹמֵעַ תְּפִלָּה

Accept our prayers, God. Hear our voices and answer us.
We praise You, God, who listens to our prayers.

Baruch ata, Adonai,	בָּרוּךְ אַתָּה, יְיָ,
shomei-a t'fila.	שׁוֹמֵעַ תְּפִלָּה.

(On weekdays, continue on page 131.)

◆◆

Shabbat is a time to rest, to pray, to play,
to be with people we love.
We remind ourselves that God created the world,
and we promise to take better care of it.

May this Shabbat bring children
closer to their parents.
May parents reach out to their children in love.

We thank You, God, for this day of rest and holiness.
On Shabbat, we feel richer and more complete.

Baruch ata, Adonai,	בָּרוּךְ אַתָּה, יי,
m'kadeish ha-Shabbat.	מְקַדֵּשׁ הַשַּׁבָּת.

Yism'chu v'malchut'cha	יִשְׂמְחוּ בְמַלְכוּתְךָ
shom'rei Shabbat	שׁוֹמְרֵי שַׁבָּת
v'kor'ei oneg.	וְקוֹרְאֵי עֹנֶג.
Am m'kad'shei sh'vi-i,	עַם מְקַדְּשֵׁי שְׁבִיעִי,
kulam yisb'u	כֻּלָּם יִשְׂבְּעוּ
v'yit-an'gu mituvecha.	וְיִתְעַנְּגוּ מִטּוּבֶךָ.
V'hash'vi-i ratzita bo	וְהַשְּׁבִיעִי רָצִיתָ בּוֹ
v'kidashto.	וְקִדַּשְׁתּוֹ.
Chemdat yamim	חֶמְדַּת יָמִים
oto karata,	אוֹתוֹ קָרָאתָ,
zeicher l'ma-asei	זֵכֶר לְמַעֲשֵׂה
v'reishit.	בְרֵאשִׁית.

◆◆

(On weekdays and Shabbat continue here.)

◆ **WORSHIP** ◆ עֲבוֹדָה

O God, may we always say and do what is right and good. Wherever we live—in this country, in the land of Israel, anywhere—may we understand that You are our God. We pray to You.

Baruch ata, Adonai,	בָּרוּךְ אַתָּה, יי,
she-ot'cha l'vad'cha	שֶׁאוֹתְךָ לְבַדְּךָ
b'yir-a na-avod.	בְּיִרְאָה נַעֲבוֹד.

◆ **THANKSGIVING** ◆ הוֹדָאָה

Source of good, thank You for Your many gifts
and blessings that fill our lives:
sweet smells, delicious tastes and warm touch;
friendship and love and life;
Your Torah, which teaches us wisdom.
We praise You, God, for all Your goodness.

Baruch ata, Adonai,	בָּרוּךְ אַתָּה, יי,
hatov shimcha ul'cha	הַטּוֹב שִׁמְךָ וּלְךָ
na-eh l'hodot.	נָאֶה לְהוֹדוֹת.

◆ PEACE ◆ בִּרְכַּת שָׁלוֹם

May Israel and all the world
enjoy peace and happiness, blessing and mercy.
Be with us, God, and we shall find
justice, peace and life.
We praise You, God, the Source of peace.

FOR AN EVENING SERVICE

Shalom rav al Yisra-eil	שָׁלוֹם רָב עַל־יִשְׂרָאֵל
am'cha tasim l'olam,	עַמְּךָ תָּשִׂים לְעוֹלָם,
ki ata hu	כִּי אַתָּה הוּא
melech adon	מֶלֶךְ אָדוֹן
l'chol hashalom.	לְכָל הַשָּׁלוֹם.
V'tov b'einecha l'vareich	וְטוֹב בְּעֵינֶיךָ לְבָרֵךְ
et am'cha Yisra-eil	אֶת־עַמְּךָ יִשְׂרָאֵל
b'chol eit uv'chol sha-a	בְּכָל־עֵת וּבְכָל־שָׁעָה
bish'lomecha.	בִּשְׁלוֹמֶךָ.
Baruch ata, Adonai,	בָּרוּךְ אַתָּה, יְיָ,
ham'vareich	הַמְבָרֵךְ
et amo Yisra-eil	אֶת־עַמּוֹ יִשְׂרָאֵל
bashalom.	בַּשָּׁלוֹם.

FOR A MORNING SERVICE

Sim shalom,	שִׂים שָׁלוֹם,
tova uv'racha,	טוֹבָה וּבְרָכָה,
chein vachesed	חֵן וָחֶסֶד
v'rachamim,	וְרַחֲמִים,
aleinu v'al	עָלֵינוּ וְעַל
kol Yisra-eil amecha.	כָּל־יִשְׂרָאֵל עַמֶּךָ.

Bar'cheinu, avinu,	בָּרְכֵנוּ אָבִינוּ,
kulanu k'echad,	כֻּלָּנוּ כְּאֶחָד,
b'or panecha,	בְּאוֹר פָּנֶיךָ,
ki v'or panecha	כִּי בְאוֹר פָּנֶיךָ
natata lanu,	נָתַתָּ לָנוּ,
Adonai Eloheinu,	יי אֱלֹהֵינוּ,
Torat chayim	תּוֹרַת חַיִּים,
v'ahavat chesed,	וְאַהֲבַת חֶסֶד,
utz'daka uv'racha	וּצְדָקָה וּבְרָכָה
v'rachamim v'chayim	וְרַחֲמִים וְחַיִּים
v'shalom.	וְשָׁלוֹם.
V'tov b'einecha l'vareich	וְטוֹב בְּעֵינֶיךָ לְבָרֵךְ
et am'cha Yisra-eil	אֶת־עַמְּךָ יִשְׂרָאֵל
v'et kol ha-amim,	וְאֶת־כָּל־הָעַמִּים,
b'chol eit uv'chol sha-a	בְּכָל־עֵת וּבְכָל־שָׁעָה
bish'lomecha.	בִּשְׁלוֹמֶךָ.
Baruch ata, Adonai,	בָּרוּךְ אַתָּה, יי,
osei hashalom.	עוֹשֵׂה הַשָּׁלוֹם.

SILENT PRAYER

(For a Torah reading, turn to page 134.)

(For Closing Prayers, turn to page 141.)

Seder K'ri-at Ha-Torah

סֵדֶר קְרִיאַת הַתּוֹרָה

Long ago, it was written in Torah: assemble the people—men, women and children, even strangers—to hear the words of Torah, to learn to love God, to do what Torah teaches.

PLEASE RISE

(Open the Ark)

Al sh'losha d'varim	עַל־שְׁלשָׁה דְבָרִים
ha-olam omeid:	הָעוֹלָם עוֹמֵד:
al ha-Torah,	עַל הַתּוֹרָה,
v'al ha-avoda,	וְעַל הָעֲבוֹדָה,
v'al g'milut chasadim.	וְעַל גְּמִילוּת חֲסָדִים.

On three things the world stands:
Torah, worship and loving deeds.

FOR ADULTS TO READ:

Torah is a tree of life we planted and cared for.
Now, we invite our children to join us.

FOR CHILDREN TO RESPOND:

We are young, but we know that Torah is special.
It is holy. We become holy when we learn from Torah
and fill our lives with its teachings.
We rise to praise God for the gift of Torah.

◆◆

Havu godel leiloheinu,	הָבוּ גֹדֶל לֵאלֹהֵינוּ,
ut'nu chavod la-Torah.	וּתְנוּ כָבוֹד לַתּוֹרָה.

Let us declare God's greatness and
give honor to the Torah.

Ki mi-Tziyon teitzei Torah,	כִּי מִצִּיּוֹן תֵּצֵא תוֹרָה,
ud'var Adonai	וּדְבַר־יהוה
mi-Yerushalayim.	מִירוּשָׁלָיִם.

Baruch shenatan Torah	בָּרוּךְ שֶׁנָּתַן תּוֹרָה
l'amo Yisra-eil	לְעַמּוֹ יִשְׂרָאֵל
bik'dushato.	בִּקְדֻשָּׁתוֹ.

In this scroll is everything that has made
the Jewish people special, from Mount Sinai until today.
Torah teaches us love and justice,
goodness and hope and freedom.

Sh'ma Yisra-eil:	שְׁמַע יִשְׂרָאֵל:
Adonai Eloheinu,	יהוה אֱלֹהֵינוּ,
Adonai echad!	יהוה אֶחָד!

Hear, O Israel,
the Eternal One is our God,
the Eternal God alone!

Echad Eloheinu,	אֶחָד אֱלֹהֵינוּ,
gadol Adoneinu,	גָּדוֹל אֲדוֹנֵינוּ,
kadosh sh'mo.	קָדוֹשׁ שְׁמוֹ.

Our God is One; our God is great;
holy is God's name.

L'cha, Adonai, hag'dula	לְךָ, יהוה, הַגְּדֻלָּה
v'hag'vura v'hatif'eret	וְהַגְּבוּרָה וְהַתִּפְאֶרֶת
v'haneitzach v'hahod,	וְהַנֵּצַח וְהַהוֹד,
ki chol bashamayim	כִּי כֹל בַּשָּׁמַיִם
uva-aretz.	וּבָאָרֶץ.
L'cha, Adonai, hamamlacha	לְךָ, יהוה, הַמַּמְלָכָה
v'hamitnasei l'chol	וְהַמִּתְנַשֵּׂא לְכֹל
l'rosh.	לְרֹאשׁ.

PLEASE BE SEATED

BLESSING BEFORE THE READING OF THE TORAH

Bar'chu et Adonai	בָּרְכוּ אֶת־יי
ham'vorach!	הַמְבֹרָךְ!
Baruch Adonai ham'vorach	בָּרוּךְ יי הַמְבֹרָךְ
l'olam va-ed!	לְעוֹלָם וָעֶד!
Baruch ata, Adonai	בָּרוּךְ אַתָּה, יי
Eloheinu, melech	אֱלֹהֵינוּ, מֶלֶךְ
ha-olam,	הָעוֹלָם,
asher bachar banu	אֲשֶׁר בָּחַר־בָּנוּ
mikol ha-amim	מִכָּל־הָעַמִּים
v'natan lanu	וְנָתַן־לָנוּ
et Torato.	אֶת־תּוֹרָתוֹ.
Baruch ata, Adonai,	בָּרוּךְ אַתָּה, יי,
notein ha-Torah.	נוֹתֵן הַתּוֹרָה.

BLESSING AFTER THE READING OF THE TORAH

Baruch ata, Adonai	בָּרוּךְ אַתָּה, יי
Eloheinu, melech	אֱלֹהֵינוּ, מֶלֶךְ
ha-olam,	הָעוֹלָם,
asher natan lanu	אֲשֶׁר נָתַן לָנוּ
Torat emet,	תּוֹרַת אֱמֶת,
v'chayei olam	וְחַיֵּי עוֹלָם
nata b'tocheinu.	נָטַע בְּתוֹכֵנוּ.
Baruch ata, Adonai,	בָּרוּךְ אַתָּה, יי,
notein ha-Torah.	נוֹתֵן הַתּוֹרָה.

(The Torah is lifted and dressed)

V'zot ha-Torah	וְזֹאת הַתּוֹרָה
asher sam Mosheh	אֲשֶׁר־שָׂם מֹשֶׁה
lifnei b'nei Yisra-eil,	לִפְנֵי בְּנֵי יִשְׂרָאֵל,
al pi Adonai	עַל־פִּי יי
b'yad Mosheh.	בְּיַד־מֹשֶׁה.

BLESSING BEFORE THE READING OF THE HAFTARAH

Baruch ata,	בָּרוּךְ אַתָּה,
Adonai Eloheinu,	יי אֱלֹהֵינוּ,
melech ha-olam,	מֶלֶךְ הָעוֹלָם,
asher bachar	אֲשֶׁר בָּחַר
bin'vi-im tovim,	בִּנְבִיאִים טוֹבִים,
v'ratza v'divreihem	וְרָצָה בְדִבְרֵיהֶם
hane-emarim be-emet.	הַנֶּאֱמָרִים בֶּאֱמֶת.
Baruch ata, Adonai,	בָּרוּךְ אַתָּה, יי,
habocheir ba-Torah,	הַבּוֹחֵר בַּתּוֹרָה,
uv'Mosheh avdo,	וּבְמֹשֶׁה עַבְדּוֹ,
uv'Yisra-eil amo,	וּבְיִשְׂרָאֵל עַמּוֹ,
uvin'vi-ei ha-emet	וּבִנְבִיאֵי הָאֱמֶת
vatzedek.	וָצֶדֶק.

Baruch ata,	בָּרוּךְ אַתָּה,
Adonai Eloheinu,	יי אֱלֹהֵינוּ,
melech ha-olam,	מֶלֶךְ הָעוֹלָם,
tzur kol ha-olamim,	צוּר כָּל־הָעוֹלָמִים,
tzadik b'chol hadorot,	צַדִּיק בְּכָל־הַדּוֹרוֹת,
ha-Eil hane-eman,	הָאֵל הַנֶּאֱמָן,
ha-omeir v'oseh,	הָאוֹמֵר וְעוֹשֶׂה,
ham'dabeir um'kayeim,	הַמְדַבֵּר וּמְקַיֵּם,
shekol d'varav	שֶׁכָּל־דְּבָרָיו
emet vatzedek.	אֱמֶת וָצֶדֶק.
Al ha-Torah v'al ha-avoda	עַל־הַתּוֹרָה וְעַל־הָעֲבוֹדָה
v'al han'vi-im	וְעַל־הַנְּבִיאִים
v'al yom ha-Shabbat hazeh,	וְעַל־יוֹם הַשַּׁבָּת הַזֶּה,
shenatata lanu,	שֶׁנָּתַתָּ־לָּנוּ,
Adonai Eloheinu,	יי אֱלֹהֵינוּ,
lik'dusha v'lim'nucha,	לִקְדֻשָּׁה וְלִמְנוּחָה,
l'chavod ul'tif-aret,	לְכָבוֹד וּלְתִפְאָרֶת,
al hakol, Adonai Eloheinu,	עַל־הַכֹּל, יי אֱלֹהֵינוּ,
anachnu modim lach	אֲנַחְנוּ מוֹדִים לָךְ
um'var'chim otach.	וּמְבָרְכִים אוֹתָךְ.
Yitbarach shimcha	יִתְבָּרַךְ שִׁמְךָ
b'fi kol chai	בְּפִי כָּל־חַי
tamid l'olam va-ed.	תָּמִיד לְעוֹלָם וָעֶד.
Baruch ata, Adonai,	בָּרוּךְ אַתָּה, יי,
m'kadeish ha-Shabbat.	מְקַדֵּשׁ הַשַּׁבָּת.

PLEASE RISE

God, let our hearts sing to You for the gift of Torah.

Hodo al eretz	הוֹדוֹ עַל־אֶרֶץ
v'shamayim,	וְשָׁמָיִם,
vayarem keren l'amo,	וַיָּרֶם קֶרֶן לְעַמּוֹ,
t'hila l'chol chasidav,	תְּהִלָּה לְכָל־חֲסִידָיו,
liv'nei Yisra-eil,	לִבְנֵי יִשְׂרָאֵל,
am k'rovo.	עַם קְרוֹבוֹ.
Halleluyah!	הַלְלוּיָהּ!

God has given us a very special gift.
Torah brings us life and happiness.
The ways of Torah are pleasing;
they lead to peace.

It is a tree of life to all who hold fast to it,
and all of its supporters are happy.

Eitz chayim hi	עֵץ־חַיִּים הִיא
lamachazikim bah,	לַמַּחֲזִיקִים בָּהּ,
v'tom'cheha m'ushar.	וְתֹמְכֶיהָ מְאֻשָּׁר.
D'racheha darchei no-am,	דְּרָכֶיהָ דַרְכֵי־נֹעַם,
v'chol n'tivoteha	וְכָל־נְתִיבוֹתֶיהָ
shalom.	שָׁלוֹם.

Hashiveinu, Adonai,	הֲשִׁיבֵנוּ, יהוה,
eilecha, v'nashuva.	אֵלֶיךָ, וְנָשׁוּבָה.
Chadeish yameinu	חַדֵּשׁ יָמֵינוּ
k'kedem.	כְּקֶדֶם.

Help us to return to You, O God; then truly shall we return.
Renew our days as in the past.

Closing Prayers

עָלֵינוּ

PLEASE RISE

Let us sing our praise to God who gives life to all creation. Your glory shines in the starry skies and in the brightness of morning. Your wonders fill our hearts and minds. We praise Adonai, the Eternal God, who has called us as partners to heal our world.

Aleinu l'shabei-ach	עָלֵינוּ לְשַׁבֵּחַ
la-adon hakol,	לַאֲדוֹן הַכֹּל,
lateit g'dula	לָתֵת גְּדֻלָּה
l'yotzeir b'reishit,	לְיוֹצֵר בְּרֵאשִׁית,
shelo asanu	שֶׁלֹּא עָשָׂנוּ
k'goyei ha-aratzot	כְּגוֹיֵי הָאֲרָצוֹת,
v'lo samanu	וְלֹא שָׂמָנוּ
k'mishp'chot ha-adama;	כְּמִשְׁפְּחוֹת הָאֲדָמָה;
shelo sam chelkeinu	שֶׁלֹּא שָׂם חֶלְקֵנוּ
kahem v'goraleinu	כָּהֶם, וְגוֹרָלֵנוּ
k'chol hamonam.	כְּכָל־הֲמוֹנָם.
Va-anachnu kor'im	וַאֲנַחְנוּ כּוֹרְעִים
umishtachavim umodim	וּמִשְׁתַּחֲוִים וּמוֹדִים
lifnei melech	לִפְנֵי מֶלֶךְ
malchei ham'lachim,	מַלְכֵי הַמְּלָכִים,
ha-Kadosh Baruch Hu.	הַקָּדוֹשׁ בָּרוּךְ הוּא.

Someday, every person will hear God's words
and do what God commands.

We pray with all our hearts:
let there be no more fighting and violence and war.
Let the time come soon
when people will be kind to each other,
when no one will be hungry or homeless,
when everyone will be free.

Let us begin.
May our love and care bring nearer the time
when all people will be one peaceful human family.
On that day, all people will say:
Adonai is the one and only God of the whole world.

Bayom hahu	בַּיּוֹם הַהוּא
yihyeh Adonai echad	יִהְיֶה יהוה אֶחָד
ush'mo echad.	וּשְׁמוֹ אֶחָד.

As our service ends, we think about people whose lives have ended. Some of them we knew, and they were very special to us; we loved them, and we miss them very much. Others we did not know, but we honor them as well.

With our Kaddish prayer,
we thank You, God, for life and love.
We remember wonderful people
and we praise You for their lives.
We, too, shall try to live as You want us to live.

Yitgadal v'yitkadash	יִתְגַּדַּל וְיִתְקַדַּשׁ
sh'mei raba	שְׁמֵהּ רַבָּא
b'alma di v'ra	בְּעָלְמָא דִּי־בְרָא
chir'utei, v'yamlich	כִרְעוּתֵהּ, וְיַמְלִיךְ
malchutei b'chayeichon	מַלְכוּתֵהּ בְּחַיֵּיכוֹן
uv'yomeichon uv'chayei	וּבְיוֹמֵיכוֹן וּבְחַיֵּי
d'chol beit Yisra-eil,	דְכָל־בֵּית יִשְׂרָאֵל,
ba-agala	בַּעֲגָלָא
uvizman kariv,	וּבִזְמַן קָרִיב,
v'imru: Amein.	וְאִמְרוּ: אָמֵן.
Y'hei sh'mei raba	יְהֵא שְׁמֵהּ רַבָּא
m'varach l'alam	מְבָרַךְ לְעָלַם
ul'almei almaya.	וּלְעָלְמֵי עָלְמַיָּא.

Yitbarach v'yishtabach,	יִתְבָּרַךְ וְיִשְׁתַּבַּח,
v'yitpa-ar v'yitromam	וְיִתְפָּאַר וְיִתְרוֹמַם
v'yitnasei,	וְיִתְנַשֵּׂא,
v'yithadar v'yit-aleh	וְיִתְהַדַּר וְיִתְעַלֶּה
v'yithalal	וְיִתְהַלַּל
sh'mei d'kud'sha,	שְׁמֵהּ דְּקוּדְשָׁא,
b'rich hu,	בְּרִיךְ הוּא,
l'eila min kol birchata	לְעֵלָּא מִן־כָּל־בִּרְכָתָא
v'shirata,	וְשִׁירָתָא,
tushb'chata v'nechemata	תֻּשְׁבְּחָתָא וְנֶחֱמָתָא
da-amiram b'alma,	דַּאֲמִירָן בְּעָלְמָא,
v'imru: Amein	וְאִמְרוּ: אָמֵן.

Y'hei sh'lama raba	יְהֵא שְׁלָמָא רַבָּא
min sh'maya	מִן־שְׁמַיָּא
v'chayim aleinu	וְחַיִּים עָלֵינוּ
v'al kol Yisra-eil,	וְעַל־כָּל־יִשְׂרָאֵל,
v'imru: Amein.	וְאִמְרוּ: אָמֵן.

Oseh shalom bim'romav,	עֹשֶׂה שָׁלוֹם בִּמְרוֹמָיו,
hu ya-aseh shalom	הוּא יַעֲשֶׂה שָׁלוֹם
aleinu v'al kol Yisra-eil,	עָלֵינוּ וְעַל כָּל־יִשְׂרָאֵל,
v'imru: Amein.	וְאִמְרוּ: אָמֵן.

CONCLUDING SONGS BEGIN ON PAGE 147.

FOR KIDDUSH, TURN TO PAGE 105.

Songs

Songs

Adon Olam 148
Al Sh'losha D'varim 149
Eileh Cham'da Libi 149
Ein Adir . . . . . see Mipi Eil
Ein Keiloheinu 150
Eitz Chayim 151
Esa Einai 151
Hinei Ma Tov 152
L'cha Dodi 152
Lo Yisa Goi 154
Ma Tovu 154
Ma Yafeh Hayom 155
Mipi Eil 155
Modeh Ani 157
Oseh Shalom 157
Shalom Aleichem 158
Shalom Rav 159
Sim Shalom 160
Tov L'hodot 161

Discover other wonderful songs in *Manginot,* the extensive collection of music for Jewish schools, and *Gates of Song,* a comprehensive selection of music for Shabbat, both published by Transcontinental Music Publications, 838 Fifth Avenue, New York, New York 10021.

אֲדוֹן עוֹלָם אֲשֶׁר מָלַךְ, בְּטֶֽרֶם כָּל־יְצִיר נִבְרָא,
לְעֵת נַעֲשָׂה בְחֶפְצוֹ כֹּל, אֲזַי מֶֽלֶךְ שְׁמוֹ נִקְרָא.

A-don o-lam a-sher ma-lach, b'te-rem kol y'tzir niv-ra,
l'eit na-a-sa v'chef-tzo kol, a-zai me-lech sh'mo nik-ra.

וְאַחֲרֵי כִּכְלוֹת הַכֹּל, לְבַדּוֹ יִמְלוֹךְ נוֹרָא;
וְהוּא הָיָה וְהוּא הֹוֶה, וְהוּא יִהְיֶה בְּתִפְאָרָה.

V'a-cha-rei kich-lot ha-kol, l'va-do yim-loch no-ra;
ve-hu ha-ya ve-hu ho-veh, ve-hu yih-yeh b'tif-a-ra.

וְהוּא אֶחָד, וְאֵין שֵׁנִי, לְהַמְשִׁיל לוֹ, לְהַחְבִּֽירָה,
בְּלִי רֵאשִׁית, בְּלִי תַכְלִית, וְלוֹ הָעֹז וְהַמִּשְׂרָה.

V'hu e-chad, v'ein shei-ni, l'ham-shil lo, l'hach-bi-ra,
b'li rei-sheet, b'li tach-lit, v'lo ha-oz v'ha-mis-ra.

וְהוּא אֵלִי, וְחַי גֹּאֲלִי, וְצוּר חֶבְלִי בְּעֵת צָרָה,
וְהוּא נִסִּי וּמָנוֹס לִי, מְנָת כּוֹסִי בְּיוֹם אֶקְרָא.

V'hu Ei-li, v'chai go-a-li, v'tzur chev-li b'eit tza-ra,
v'hu ni-si u-ma-nos li, m'nat ko-si b'yom ek-ra.

בְּיָדוֹ אַפְקִיד רוּחִי, בְּעֵת אִישַׁן וְאָעִֽירָה,
וְעִם־רוּחִי גְּוִיָּתִי; יי לִי, וְלֹא אִירָא.

B'ya-do af-kid ru-chi, b'eit i-shan v'a-i-ra,
v'im ru-chi g'vi-ya-ti; A-do-nai li, v'lo i-ra.

You are the Eternal, who reigned before any being had been created. When all was done according to Your will, already then You were called Ruler.

AL SH'LOSHA D'VARIM — עַל־שְׁלשָׁה דְבָרִים

Al sh'lo-sha d'va-rim	עַל־שְׁלשָׁה דְבָרִים
ha-o-lam o-meid:	הָעוֹלָם עוֹמֵד:
al ha-To-rah,	עַל הַתּוֹרָה,
v'al ha-a-vo-da,	וְעַל הָעֲבוֹדָה,
v'al g'mi-lut cha-sa-dim.	וְעַל גְּמִילוּת חֲסָדִים.

On three things the world stands:
Torah, worship and loving deeds.

EILEH CHAM'DA LIBI — אֵלֶּה חָמְדָה לִבִּי

Ei-leh cha-m'da li-bi:	אֵלֶּה חָמְדָה לִבִּי:
chu-sa na v'al na	חוּסָה נָּא וְאַל נָא
tit-a-leim.	תִּתְעַלֵּם.

This is my heart's desire: have pity, do not hide Yourself!

אֵין כֵּאלֹהֵינוּ, אֵין כַּאדוֹנֵינוּ,
אֵין כְּמַלְכֵּנוּ, אֵין כְּמוֹשִׁיעֵנוּ.

Ein kei-lo-hei-nu, ein ka-do-nei-nu,
ein k'mal-kei-nu, ein k'mo-shi-ei-nu.

מִי כֵאלֹהֵינוּ? מִי כַאדוֹנֵינוּ?
מִי כְמַלְכֵּנוּ? מִי כְמוֹשִׁיעֵנוּ?

Mi chei-lo-hei-nu? Mi cha-do-nei-nu?
Mi ch'mal-kei-nu? Mi ch'mo-shi-ei-nu?

נוֹדֶה לֵאלֹהֵינוּ, נוֹדֶה לַאדוֹנֵינוּ,
נוֹדֶה לְמַלְכֵּנוּ, נוֹדֶה לְמוֹשִׁיעֵנוּ.

No-deh lei-lo-hei-nu, no-deh la-do-nei-nu,
no-deh l'mal-kei-nu, no-deh l'mo-shi-ei-nu.

בָּרוּךְ אֱלֹהֵינוּ, בָּרוּךְ אֲדוֹנֵינוּ,
בָּרוּךְ מַלְכֵּנוּ, בָּרוּךְ מוֹשִׁיעֵנוּ.

Ba-ruch E-lo-hei-nu, ba-ruch A-do-nei-nu,
ba-ruch Mal-kei-nu, ba-ruch Mo-shi-ei-nu.

אַתָּה הוּא אֱלֹהֵינוּ, אַתָּה הוּא אֲדוֹנֵינוּ,
אַתָּה הוּא מַלְכֵּנוּ, אַתָּה הוּא מוֹשִׁיעֵנוּ.

A-ta hu E-lo-hei-nu, a-ta hu A-do-nei-nu,
a-ta hu Mal-kei-nu, a-ta hu Mo-shi-ei-nu.

There is none like our God, our Sovereign, our Redeemer.
Who is like our God, our Sovereign, our Redeemer?
We give thanks to our God, our Sovereign, our Redeemer.
You are our God, our Sovereign, our Redeemer.
Praised be our God, our Sovereign, our Redeemer.

◆ EITZ CHAYIM ◆ עֵץ חַיִּים

Eitz cha-yim hi,	עֵץ־חַיִּים הִיא
la-ma-cha-zi-kim bah,	לַמַּחֲזִיקִים בָּהּ,
v'to-m'che-ha m'u-shar.	וְתֹמְכֶיהָ מְאֻשָּׁר.
D'ra-che-ha	דְּרָכֶיהָ
dar-chei no-am,	דַרְכֵי־נֹעַם,
v'chol n'ti-vo-te-ha sha-lom.	וְכָל־נְתִיבוֹתֶיהָ שָׁלוֹם.
Ha-shi-vei-nu, A-do-nai,	הֲשִׁיבֵנוּ, יהוה,
ei-le-cha, v'na-shu-va.	אֵלֶיךָ, וְנָשׁוּבָה.
Cha-deish ya-mei-nu	חַדֵּשׁ יָמֵינוּ
k'ke-dem.	כְּקֶדֶם.

It is a tree of life to those who hold it fast, and all who cling to it find happiness. Its ways are ways of pleasantness, and all its paths are peace. Help us to return to You, O God; then truly shall we return. Renew our days as in the past.

◆ ESA EINAI ◆ אֶשָּׂא עֵינַי

E-sa ei-nai el he-ha-rim,	אֶשָּׂא עֵינַי אֶל־הֶהָרִים,
mei-a-yin ya-vo ez-ri?	מֵאַיִן יָבוֹא עֶזְרִי?
Ez-ri mei-im Adonai,	עֶזְרִי מֵעִם יהוה,
o-sei sha-ma-yim va-a-retz.	עֹשֵׂה שָׁמַיִם וָאָרֶץ.

I lift up my eyes unto the mountains,
From where does my help come?
My help comes from God,
Maker of heaven and earth.

HINEI MA TOV ◆ הִנֵּה מַה טּוֹב

Hi-nei ma tov	הִנֵּה מַה־טּוֹב
u-ma na-im	וּמַה־נָּעִים
she-vet a-chim	שֶׁבֶת אַחִים
gam ya-chad.	גַּם־יָחַד.

How good and pleasant it is
for brothers and sisters to sit together.

L'CHA DODI ◆ לְכָה דוֹדִי

לְכָה דוֹדִי לִקְרַאת כַּלָּה, פְּנֵי שַׁבָּת נְקַבְּלָה.
לְכָה דוֹדִי לִקְרַאת כַּלָּה, פְּנֵי שַׁבָּת נְקַבְּלָה.

L'cha do-di lik-rat ka-la, p'nei sha-bat n'ka-b'la.
L'cha do-di lik-rat ka-la, p'nei sha-bat n'ka-b'la.

שָׁמוֹר וְזָכוֹר בְּדִבּוּר אֶחָד,
הִשְׁמִיעָנוּ אֵל הַמְיֻחָד.
יי אֶחָד וּשְׁמוֹ אֶחָד,
לְשֵׁם וּלְתִפְאֶרֶת וְלִתְהִלָּה.

Sha-mor v'za-chor b'di-bur e-chad,
hish-mi-a-nu Eil ha-m'yu-chad.
A-do-nai e-chad u-sh'mo e-chad,
l'sheim u-l'tif-e-ret v'li-t'hi-la.

לְכָה דוֹדִי . . .

L'cha do-di . . .

הִתְעוֹרְרִי, הִתְעוֹרְרִי,
כִּי בָא אוֹרֵךְ! קוּמִי, אוֹרִי,
עוּרִי עוּרִי, שִׁיר דַּבֵּרִי;
כְּבוֹד יי עָלַיִךְ נִגְלָה.

Hit-o-r'ri, hit-o-r'ri,
ki va o-reich! Ku-mi, o-ri,
u-ri u-ri, shir da-bei-ri;
k'vod A-do-nai a-la-yich nig-la.

לְכָה דוֹדִי . . .

L'cha do-di . . .

בּוֹאִי בְשָׁלוֹם, עֲטֶרֶת בַּעְלָהּ;
גַּם בְּשִׂמְחָה וּבְצָהֳלָה.
תּוֹךְ אֱמוּנֵי עַם סְגֻלָּה.
בּוֹאִי כַלָּה! בּוֹאִי כַלָּה!

Bo-i v'sha-lom, a-te-ret ba-a-lah;
gam b'sim-cha u-v'tso-ho-la,
toch e-mu-nei am s'gu-la.
Bo-i cha-la! Bo-i cha-la!

לְכָה דוֹדִי . . .

L'cha do-di . . .

Beloved, come to meet the bride;
beloved, come to greet Shabbat.

Keep and remember: a single command,
the Only God caused us to hear;
the Eternal is One, God's name is One,
for honor and glory and praise.

Awake, awake, your light has come!
Arise, shine, awake and sing;
the Eternal's glory dawns upon you.

Enter in peace, O crown of your husband; enter in gladness,
enter in joy. Come to the people that keeps its faith.
Enter, O bride! Enter, O bride!

◆ LO YISA GOI ◆ לֹא יִשָּׂא גוֹי

Lo yi-sa goi el goi che-rev	לֹא יִשָּׂא גוֹי אֶל גּוֹי חֶרֶב,
lo yil-m'du od	לֹא יִלְמְדוּ עוֹד
mil-cha-ma.	מִלְחָמָה.

Nation shall not lift up sword against nation,
nor ever again shall they train for war.

◆ MA TOVU ◆ מַה־טֹּבוּ

מַה־טֹּבוּ אֹהָלֶיךָ, יַעֲקֹב,
מִשְׁכְּנֹתֶיךָ, יִשְׂרָאֵל!

Ma to-vu o-ha-le-cha, Ya-a-kov,
mish-k'no-te-cha, Yis-ra-eil!

וַאֲנִי, בְּרֹב חַסְדְּךָ אָבוֹא בֵיתֶךָ,
אֶשְׁתַּחֲוֶה אֶל־הֵיכַל קָדְשְׁךָ בְּיִרְאָתֶךָ.

Va-a-ni b'rov chas-d'cha a-vo vei-te-cha,
esh-ta-cha-veh el hei-chal kod-sh'cha b'yir-a-te-cha.

יי, אָהַבְתִּי מְעוֹן בֵּיתֶךָ,
וּמְקוֹם מִשְׁכַּן כְּבוֹדֶךָ.
וַאֲנִי אֶשְׁתַּחֲוֶה וְאֶכְרָעָה,
אֶבְרְכָה לִפְנֵי־יי עֹשִׂי.

A-do-nai, a-hav-ti m'on bei-te-cha,
u-m'kom mish-kan k'vo-de-cha.
Va-a-ni esh-ta-cha-veh v'ech-ra-a,
ev-r'cha li-f'nei A-do-nai o-si.

וַאֲנִי תְפִלָּתִי לְךָ,
יי, עֵת רָצוֹן.
אֱלֹהִים, בְּרָב־חַסְדֶּךָ,
עֲנֵנִי בֶּאֱמֶת יִשְׁעֶךָ.

Va-a-ni t'fi-la-ti l'cha,
A-do-nai, eit ra-tzon.
E-lo-him, b'rov chas-de-cha,
A-nei-ni be-e-met yish-e-cha.

How lovely are your tents, O Jacob,
your dwelling places, O Israel.

◆ MA YAFEH HAYOM ◆ מַה יָּפֶה הַיּוֹם

מַה יָּפֶה הַיּוֹם,
שַׁבָּת שָׁלוֹם.

Ma ya-feh ha-yom,
Sha-bat sha-lom.

How beautiful is this day. Shabbat shalom.

◆ MIPI EIL ◆ מִפִּי אֵל

אֵין אַדִּיר כַּיי
וְאֵין בָּרוּךְ
כְּבֶן עַמְרָם.
אֵין גְּדוֹלָה כַּתּוֹרָה
וְאֵין דַּרְשָׁנֶיהָ
כְּיִשְׂרָאֵל.

Ein a-dir ka-do-nai
v'ein ba-ruch
k'ven Am-ram.
Ein g'do-la ka-To-rah
v'ein dar-sha-ne-ha
k'Yis-ra-eil.

מִפִּי אֵל וּמִפִּי אֵל
יְבֹרַךְ כָּל יִשְׂרָאֵל.

Mi-pi Eil u-mi-pi Eil
y'vo-rach kol Yis-ra-eil.

Ein ha-dur ka-do-nai	אֵין הָדוּר כַּיי
v'ein va-tik	וְאֵין וָתִיק
k'ven Am-ram.	כְּבֶן עַמְרָם.
Ein za-ka ka-To-rah	אֵין זַכָּה כַּתּוֹרָה
v'ein cha-cha-me-ha	וְאֵין חֲכָמֶיהָ
k'Yis-ra-eil.	כְּיִשְׂרָאֵל.
Mi-pi Eil u-mi-pi Eil	מִפִּי אֵל וּמִפִּי אֵל
y'vo-rach kol Yis-ra-eil.	יְבֹרַךְ כָּל יִשְׂרָאֵל.
Ein ta-hor ka-do-nai	אֵין טָהוֹר כַּיי
v'ein ya-chid	וְאֵין יָחִיד
k'ven Am-ram.	כְּבֶן עַמְרָם.
Ein ka-bi-ra ka-To-rah	אֵין כַּבִּירָה כַּתּוֹרָה
v'ein lam-da-ne-ha	וְאֵין לַמְדָנֶיהָ
k'Yis-ra-eil.	כְּיִשְׂרָאֵל.
Mi-pi Eil . . .	מִפִּי אֵל . . .
Ein po-deh ka-do-nai	אֵין פּוֹדֶה כַּיי
v'ein tza-dik	וְאֵין צַדִּיק
k'ven Am-ram.	כְּבֶן עַמְרָם.
Ein k'do-sha ka-To-rah	אֵין קְדוֹשָׁה כַּתּוֹרָה
v'ein to-m'che-ha	וְאֵין תּוֹמְכֶיהָ
k'Yis-ra-eil.	כְּיִשְׂרָאֵל.
Mi-pi Eil . . .	מִפִּי אֵל . . .

None is mighty as the Eternal; none so blessed as Amram's son; nothing is as great as the Torah; none can interpret it as Israel can. From the mouth of God, let all Israel be blessed.

◆ MODEH ANI ◆ מוֹדֶה אֲנִי

Mo-deh a-ni l'fa-ne-cha,	מוֹדֶה אֲנִי לְפָנֶיךָ,
Me-lech chai v'ka-yam,	מֶלֶךְ חַי וְקַיָּם,
sheh-he-che-zar-ta bi	שֶׁהֶחֱזַרְתָּ בִּי
nish-ma-ti b'chem-la;	נִשְׁמָתִי בְּחֶמְלָה;
ra-ba e-mu-na-te-cha.	רַבָּה אֱמוּנָתֶךָ.

I give thanks to You, O God, Eternal and living ruler, who in mercy has returned my soul to me; great is Your faithfulness.

◆ OSEH SHALOM ◆ עֹשֶׂה שָׁלוֹם

O-seh sha-lom bi-m'ro-mav,	עֹשֶׂה שָׁלוֹם בִּמְרוֹמָיו,
hu ya-a-seh sha-lom	הוּא יַעֲשֶׂה שָׁלוֹם
a-lei-nu v'al kol Yis-ra-eil,	עָלֵינוּ וְעַל כָּל־יִשְׂרָאֵל,
v'im-ru: A-mein.	וְאִמְרוּ: אָמֵן.

May the One who causes peace to reign in the high heavens, let peace descend on us, on all Israel, and all the world, and let us say: Amen.

◆ SHALOM ALEICHEM ◆ שָׁלוֹם עֲלֵיכֶם

Sha-lom a-lei-chem,	שָׁלוֹם עֲלֵיכֶם,
mal-a-chei ha-sha-reit,	מַלְאֲכֵי הַשָּׁרֵת,
mal-a-chei el-yon,	מַלְאֲכֵי עֶלְיוֹן,
mi-me-lech	מִמֶּלֶךְ
ma-l'chei ha-m'la-chim,	מַלְכֵי הַמְּלָכִים,
ha-ka-dosh ba-ruch hu.	הַקָּדוֹשׁ בָּרוּךְ הוּא.
Bo-a-chem l'sha-lom,	בּוֹאֲכֶם לְשָׁלוֹם,
mal-a-chei ha-sha-lom,	מַלְאֲכֵי הַשָּׁלוֹם,
mal-a-chei el-yon,	מַלְאֲכֵי עֶלְיוֹן,
mi-me-lech	מִמֶּלֶךְ
ma-l'chei ha-m'la-chim,	מַלְכֵי הַמְּלָכִים,
ha-ka-dosh ba-ruch hu.	הַקָּדוֹשׁ בָּרוּךְ הוּא.
Ba-r'chu-ni l'sha-lom,	בָּרְכוּנִי לְשָׁלוֹם,
mal-a-chei ha-sha-lom,	מַלְאֲכֵי הַשָּׁלוֹם,
mal-a-chei el-yon,	מַלְאֲכֵי עֶלְיוֹן,
mi-me-lech	מִמֶּלֶךְ
ma-l'chei ha-m'la-chim,	מַלְכֵי הַמְּלָכִים,
ha-ka-dosh ba-ruch hu.	הַקָּדוֹשׁ בָּרוּךְ הוּא.
Tzei-t'chem l'sha-lom,	צֵאתְכֶם לְשָׁלוֹם,
mal-a-chei ha-sha-lom,	מַלְאֲכֵי הַשָּׁלוֹם,
mal-a-chei el-yon,	מַלְאֲכֵי עֶלְיוֹן,
mi-me-lech	מִמֶּלֶךְ
ma-l'chei ha-m'la-chim,	מַלְכֵי הַמְּלָכִים,
ha-ka-dosh ba-ruch hu.	הַקָּדוֹשׁ בָּרוּךְ הוּא.

Peace be to you, O ministering angels, messengers of the Most High, the supreme Ruler of rulers, the Holy One of blessing.

שָׁלוֹם רָב עַל־יִשְׂרָאֵל עַמְּךָ תָּשִׂים לְעוֹלָם,
כִּי אַתָּה הוּא מֶלֶךְ אָדוֹן לְכָל־הַשָּׁלוֹם.
וְטוֹב בְּעֵינֶיךָ לְבָרֵךְ אֶת־עַמְּךָ יִשְׂרָאֵל
בְּכָל־עֵת וּבְכָל־שָׁעָה בִּשְׁלוֹמֶךָ.
בָּרוּךְ אַתָּה, יְיָ,
הַמְבָרֵךְ אֶת־עַמּוֹ יִשְׂרָאֵל בַּשָּׁלוֹם.

Sha-lom rav al Yis-ra-eil a-m'cha ta-sim l'o-lam,
ki a-ta hu me-lech a-don l'chol ha-sha-lom.
V'tov b'ei-ne-cha l'va-reich et a-m'cha Yis-ra-eil
b'chol eit u-v'chol sha-a bi-sh'lo-me-cha.
Ba-ruch a-ta, Adonai,
ha-m'va-reich et a-mo Yis-ra-eil ba-sha-lom.

May God always give great peace to Your people Israel.
It is good in Your sight always to bless
Your people Israel with peace.

Sim sha-lom,	שִׂים שָׁלוֹם,
to-va uv'ra-cha,	טוֹבָה וּבְרָכָה,
chein va-che-sed v'ra-cha-mim,	חֵן וָחֶסֶד וְרַחֲמִים,
a-lei-nu v'al kol Yis-ra-eil	עָלֵינוּ וְעַל כָּל־יִשְׂרָאֵל
a-me-cha.	עַמֶּךָ.
Ba-r'chei-nu a-vi-nu,	בָּרְכֵנוּ אָבִינוּ,
ku-la-nu k'e-chad,	כֻּלָּנוּ כְּאֶחָד,
b'or pa-ne-cha,	בְּאוֹר פָּנֶיךָ,
ki v'or pa-ne-cha	כִּי בְאוֹר פָּנֶיךָ
na-ta-ta la-nu,	נָתַתָּ לָּנוּ,
Adonai E-lo-hei-nu,	יי אֱלֹהֵינוּ,
to-rat cha-yim,	תּוֹרַת חַיִּים,
v'a-ha-vat che-sed,	וְאַהֲבַת חֶסֶד,
u-tz'da-ka u-v'ra-cha	וּצְדָקָה וּבְרָכָה
v'ra-cha-mim v'cha-yim	וְרַחֲמִים וְחַיִּים
v'sha-lom.	וְשָׁלוֹם.
V'tov b'ei-ne-cha l'va-reich	וְטוֹב בְּעֵינֶיךָ לְבָרֵךְ
et a-m'cha Yis-ra-eil	אֶת־עַמְּךָ יִשְׂרָאֵל
b'chol eit u-v'chol sha-a	בְּכָל־עֵת וּבְכָל־שָׁעָה
bi-sh'lo-me-cha.	בִּשְׁלוֹמֶךָ.
Ba-ruch a-ta, Adonai,	בָּרוּךְ אַתָּה, יי,
ha-m'va-reich et a-mo	הַמְבָרֵךְ אֶת־עַמּוֹ
Yis-ra-eil ba-sha-lom.	יִשְׂרָאֵל בַּשָּׁלוֹם.

Grant peace, happiness, blessing, goodness and mercy to us and Your people Israel.

◆ TOV L'HODOT I ◆ טוֹב לְהֹדוֹת – א׳

Tov, tov, tov l'ho-dot,	טוֹב, טוֹב, טוֹב לְהֹדוֹת,
tov l'ho-dot la-do-nai.	טוֹב לְהֹדוֹת לַיהוה.
U-l'za-meir l'shi-m'cha	וּלְזַמֵּר לְשִׁמְךָ
El-yon, l'shi-m'cha El-yon.	עֶלְיוֹן, לְשִׁמְךָ עֶלְיוֹן.
Tov, tov . . .	טוֹב, טוֹב . . .
L'ha-gid ba-bo-ker	לְהַגִּיד בַּבֹּקֶר
chas-de-cha,	חַסְדֶּךָ,
ve-e-mu-na-t'cha ba-lei-lot.	וֶאֱמוּנָתְךָ בַּלֵּילוֹת.
Tov, tov . . .	טוֹב, טוֹב . . .

It is good to give thanks to the Eternal,
to sing praises to Your name, O Most High!

◆ TOV L'HODOT II ◆ טוֹב לְהֹדוֹת – ב׳

Miz-mor shir	מִזְמוֹר שִׁיר
l'yom ha-Sha-bat.	לְיוֹם הַשַּׁבָּת.
Tov l'ho-dot la-do-nai	טוֹב לְהֹדוֹת לַיהוה
u-l'za-meir le-shi-m'cha	וּלְזַמֵּר לְשִׁמְךָ
El-yon.	עֶלְיוֹן.
L'ha-gid ba-bo-ker	לְהַגִּיד בַּבֹּקֶר
chas-de-cha,	חַסְדֶּךָ,
ve-e-mu-na-t'cha ba-lei-lot.	וֶאֱמוּנָתְךָ בַּלֵּילוֹת.
A-lei a-sor va-a-lei	עֲלֵי־עָשׂוֹר וַעֲלֵי־
na-vel, a-lei hi-ga-yon	נָבֶל, עֲלֵי הִגָּיוֹן
b'chi-nor.	בְּכִנּוֹר.

It is good to give thanks to the Eternal,
to sing praises to Your name, O Most High!

בָּרוּךְ